FOR
BREW
FRE
&BEA
GEEK

V

ÅKS

N

S ...

Editor
Selena Young

Editorial team
Abi Manning
Jane Rakison
Rosanna Rothery
Melissa Stewart

Editorial director
Jo Rees

Design
Tom Hampton
Dale Stiling

Community manager
Owen Penrice

Publishing
Charlotte Cummins
Tamsin Powell

Managing director
Nick Cooper

Cover image Federal Cafe & Bar
©Memphis Medium

Big thanks to the *Indy Coffee Guide* committee (meet them on page 14) for their expertise and enthusiasm, and to our partners: Cakesmiths, Cheshire Coffee Company and KeepCup.

Coffee shops, cafes and roasteries are invited to be included in the guide based on reaching criteria set by the committee, which includes using speciality beans, providing a high-quality coffee experience for visitors and being independently run.

For information on *Indy Coffee Guides* visit:

indycoffee.guide

indycoffeeguide

© Salt Media
Published by Salt Media, 2025
saltmedia.co.uk | 01271 859299
ideas@saltmedia.co.uk

salt

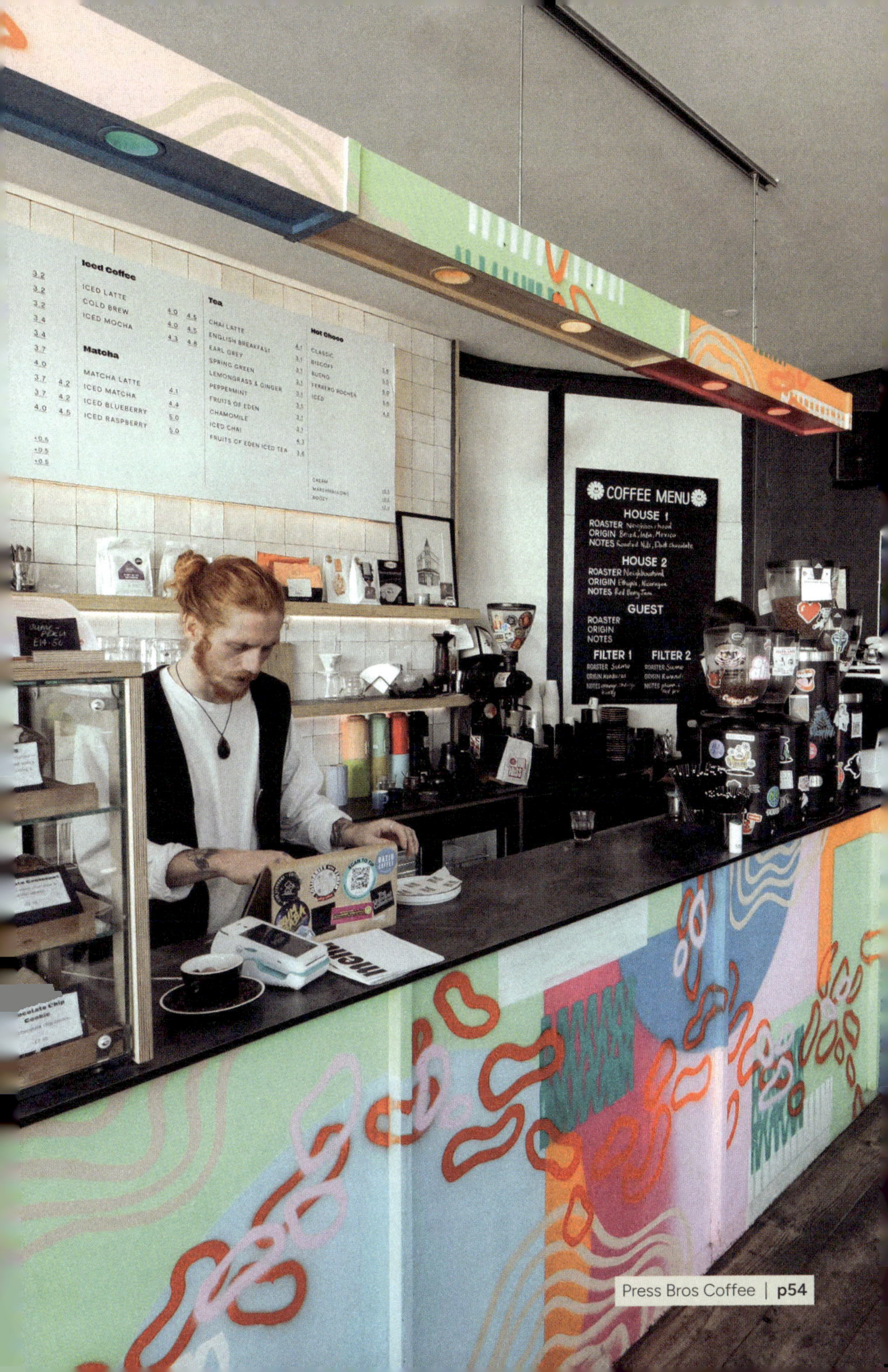

Press Bros Coffee | p54

COFFEE
FOR HOME
FILTER
BREWING

Rabbit Hole Coffee | p121

Contents

WELCOME

With 158 speciality cafes, coffee shops and roasteries featured in this new *Indy Coffee Guide North, Midlands & East England*, you're holding a passport to some super stimulating adventures in coffee.

Whether you're up for the challenge of ticking off every cafe in the guide, want to fuel a roadtrip through a particular region, or plan to hit up as many speciality coffee spots as possible in a particular city, you're armed with all the info you need.

To help you keep tabs on where you've visited and where is still waiting to be discovered, we've added a new tick box on each cafe page. Roastery pages feature a tick box too, so you can keep a record of which roasteries' beans you've tried and tested.

With the creation of each new guide we bid farewell to fun-while-it-lasted fads, find comfort in ever-faithful pairings (flat whites x cinnamon buns forever) and discover fresh coffee trends.

So thumb through this guide's pages to learn of the cafes leaning into this era of sourdough baking, and brews served in locally crafted ceramic cups. You'll also stumble over coffee-shop running clubs and discover roasteries hosting after-hours events. The trend for 'coffice' work and coffee spaces continues, while more cafes are offering a smorgasbord of rare coffees via frozen bean menus. And *whispers* if you need a break from coffee, you'll find a few swan-adorned matcha lattes in the mix too.

There are always exciting changes afoot in the speciality coffee world – it's baked into the dynamic independent scene.

Enjoy your coffee adventuring!

Selena Young

Editor

indycoffeeguide

'It's baked into the dynamic independent coffee scene'

Meet the
COMMITTEE

The *Indy Coffee Guide* team work with a crew of industry experts to identify the best cafes and roasteries to feature in the guide

Dave Olejnik

Having always sought out great coffee shops, it was during Dave's time living in Seattle (where he worked as a touring guitar tech) that he was inspired to fully divert his energy into coffee. He returned to the UK and worked for Coffee Community, travelling the world as a trainer and consultant before launching the pioneering Laynes in Leeds in 2011.

Ruth Elkington

Creativity is the golden thread running through speciality coffee businesses, a quality Ruth brings to her role as founder and director of Roost Coffee & Roastery. Utilising her degree in fashion marketing and design, and 14 years' experience in the coffee industry, Ruth weaves artistry into everything from new products to social campaigns. She launched Roost in Malton with her husband David in 2015 and it's grown into a roastery of note.

Caspar Steel

Caspar is co-director of Atkinsons Coffee Roasters, Lancaster's 186-year-old coffee roastery and collection of speciality cafes. The Steel family took over the business in 2005 and have a long-established pedigree in the industry. The pioneering team are renowned for their innovation and stay ahead of the curve in the ever-evolving speciality coffee sector.

Matthew Wade

Matthew trained as a barista and roaster in New Zealand. He brought his coffee experience with him when he returned to London, which led to him playing a leading role in the burgeoning UK coffee scene of the early noughties. Matthew became one of the UK's first Q graders and won several awards for his coffees when he was head roaster at Union Hand-Roasted, and Bullet Coffee. He set up Nightjar Coffee in 2013 in Dubai and Hundred House Coffee in 2016 in Shropshire, both multi-award-winning roasteries.

Meet the
COMMITTEE

Paul Meikle-Janney

Paul is a founder of Dark Woods Coffee, the multi-award-winning and B Corp roastery on the outskirts of Huddersfield.

In 1999, Paul started Coffee Community, an international training and consultancy agency for the speciality industry. He's co-written both the City & Guilds and SCA barista qualifications and has been involved in the World Barista Championships and UK Barista Championships since their inception.

Holly Kragiopoulos

Holly is co-founder of North Star Coffee Roasters – a B Corp-certified roastery established in Leeds in 2013 – and has worked within the speciality coffeeverse for 12 years. She became a licensed Q Grader in 2014 and participated in the international jury for the Cup of Excellence. In her role at North Star, Holly focuses on the ethical procurement of green coffee and company growth.

David Nickerson-Smith

Self-professed 'coffee handyman' David was a musician and sound engineer (a career highlight included working on *The Basil Brush Show*) before he sidestepped into speciality. After a couple of years' coffee industry experience, David opened Quaff (with the help of his wife and daughter) in Beccles, East Anglia. In 2023 he closed the cafe and now operates Full Cup Coffee Co, which supplies beans and machines to coffee shops and provides training, support and consultancy.

Jack Foster

For over a decade Jack, co-owner of Crosby Coffee Roasters, has been an authoritative voice on speciality coffee. With a successful roastery and multiple coffee shops under the Crosby brand, his aim to put Liverpool on the speciality map has come to fruition. Crosby supplies hundreds of cafes, restaurants and hotels with its ethically sourced beans, while also delivering first-rate training and education.

What's special about
SPECIALITY
COFFEE?

Speciality coffee beans are those graded above 80 on a 100-point scale (set by the Speciality Coffee Association) for quality.

👍 **80** ⟷ **100**

These beans often come from small farms across the world's coffee-growing belt, and are cultivated in select altitudes and climates by farmers who nurture the crops with great attention to detail. Q graders assess these coffees, determining if they make the grade to be classed as speciality.

The Clubhouse Roasters

Red Bank Coffee Roasters

Once speciality beans land at roasteries in the UK, they're roasted lightly to preserve the specific characteristics that are the result of the terroir in which they were grown. Roasters identify the flavours in the coffee they've roasted using a method called cupping.

Speciality green coffee beans are significantly more expensive to source than regular commodity coffee, so are treated with great care by baristas: grinding, brewing and serving the beans in a way that respects the journey from origin to cup.

Rabbit Hole Coffee

How to use the GUIDE.

Coffee shops

We've split the guide into three geographical areas to help you find speciality coffee spots to visit.

In each area, discover full-page and shot-size write-ups of coffee shops and cafes where you can drink first-rate brews.

Don't forget to tick the Been There roundel at the top of each page after you've visited a venue.

Roasteries

Meet leading speciality coffee roasters and discover where to source beans. Find them after the coffee shops in each area.

Use the Sipped That roundel at the top of each page to keep track of which roasteries' beans you've sampled.

Maps

Cafes and roasteries are numbered and marked on the map at the start of each section.

Follow us on Instagram
 indycoffeeguide

KEY

Symbols at the bottom of each cafe and roastery page provide further information on what you'll find at the venue.

Wifi	
Dogs welcome	
Bike friendly	
Reusables accepted	
Buy beans in store	
Buy beans online	
Outdoor seating	
Cafe at the roastery	
Roastery open to the public	
Roastery visit by invite	
Coffee courses	
One of multiple sites	

COFFEE
ON THE
CRESCENT

'igin Ethiopia
oaster Darkwoods
Process Anaerobic
            natural
Tasting   Black forest
notes   fruit with
           a chocolate
           finish

COFFEE
ON THE
CRESCENT

Origin El salvador
Roaster North Star
Process Washed
Tasting
notes   Plum
         Caramel
         Tangerine

COFFEE
ON THE
CRESCENT

YOUR ADVEN-TURES

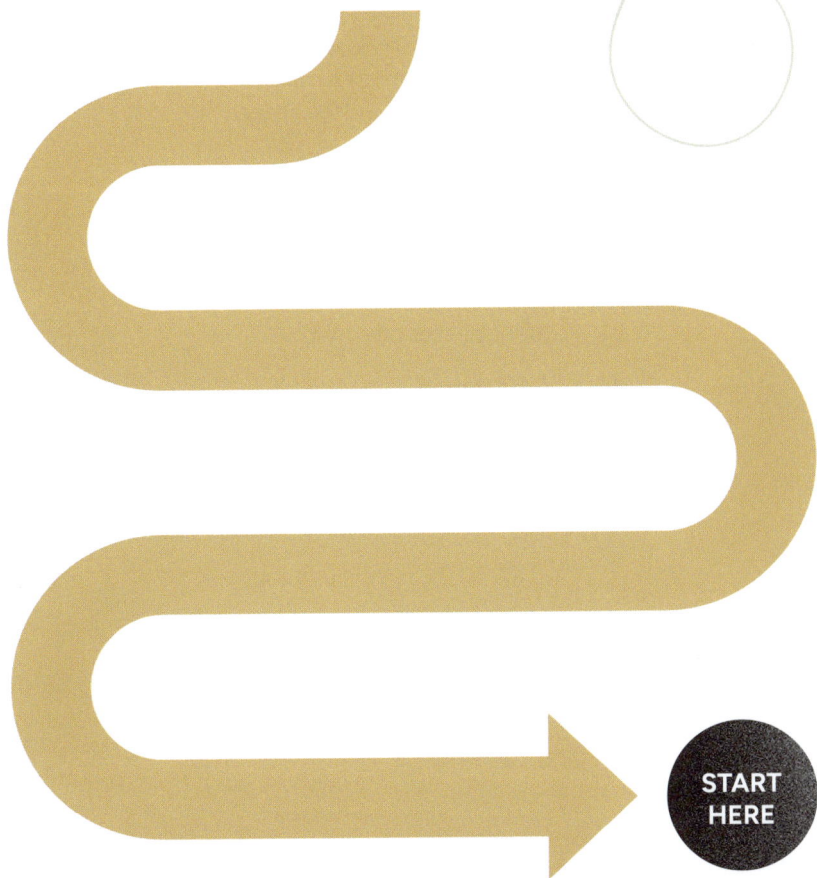

START HERE

Maps

We've split the guide into areas, grouping together neighbouring towns, cities and counties to make it easier for you to find coffee shops and roasteries.

Locations are approximate

1

Kendal

Lancaster

Preston

Liverpool

Manchester

Chester

Shrewsbury

Birmingham

Worcester

Newcastle

Middlesbrough

Whitby

Scarborough

2

Leeds

York

Hull

Sheffield

Lincoln

Nottingham

3

Leicester

Peterborough

Norwich

Bury St Edmunds

AREA

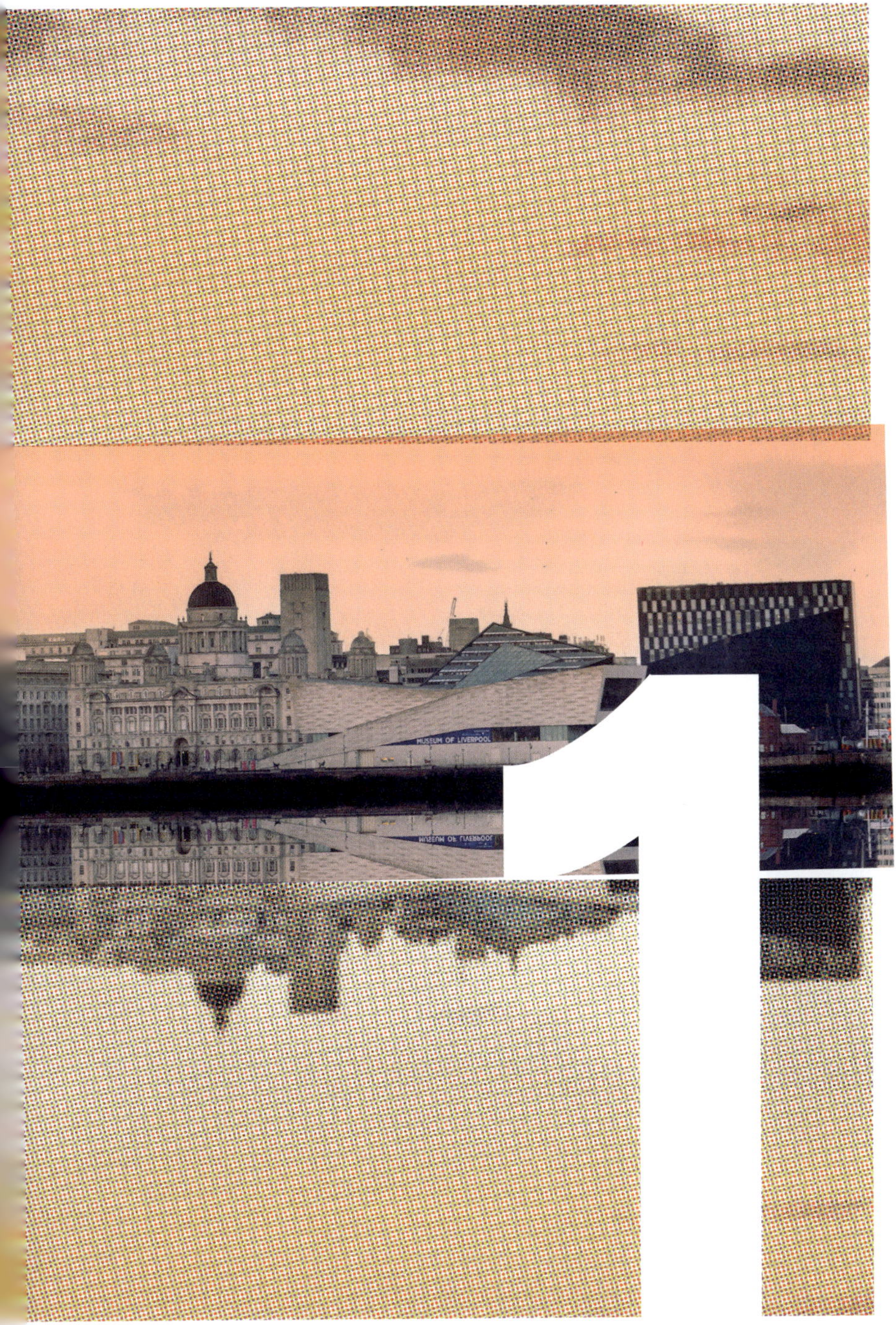
MUSEUM OF LIVERPOOL
1

Area 1

● Coffee shops

1	Marra
2	Comida [food]
3	98 Highgate
4	Homeground Coffee + Kitchen
5	Fold
6	Atkinsons The Hall
7	Atkinsons The Castle
8	Journey Social
9	Rise – Preston
10	Cedarwood Coffee Co.
11	Four1Two
12	Siphon
13	Two Brothers – Ormskirk
14	Crosby Coffee – Hightown
15-23	*See Liverpool city map on p30*
24	Two Brothers – Warrington
25	Bean & Cole
26	Tatton Perk
27	Two Brothers – Altrincham
28	Federal – Coffee Cart
29	Oscillate Coffee
30	SWIG
31	SMOAK
32	Hikari Koffee
33	Something More Productive
34-42	*See Manchester city map on p31*
43	The Frostery Living
44	Weaver & Wilde
45	Dandelion

● Roasteries

46	Rinaldo's Speciality Coffee & Fine Teas
47	Podda & Wren Coffee Roasters
48	Red Bank Coffee Roasters
49	Atkinsons Coffee Roasters
50-51	*See Liverpool city map on p30*
52	Two Brothers – Roastery
53	Oddy Knocky Coffee
54	Bohee Coffee
55	*See Manchester city map on p31*
56	Kickback Coffee

Locations are approximate

North Pennines
National Landscape

Lake District
National Park

5

3 48

4 **2** 47

Windermere

1 46

Kendal

Yorkshire
Dales
National Park

Barrow-in-Furness

8

7

Morecambe Bay

6 49

LANCASTER

Settle

Forest of
Bowland
National
Landscape

Fleetwood

Blackpool

Clitheroe

10

Preston

9

Ribble Estuary

Blackburn

Burnley

11

12 **Rawtenstall**

Chorley

Hightown

13

Bolton

33

43 **Delph**

14

Ormskirk

Wigan

53

32

44 **Uppermill**

Stretford

54 **31**

LIVERPOOL
(See city map on p30)

52

Urmston

29

30

MANCHESTER
(See city map on p31)

15-23 50-51

24

34-42 56

River Mersey

Warrington

27 **28**

River Dee

Altrincham

26

56 **Pott Shrigley**

CHESTER

Knutsford

25

45 **Buxton**

Northwich

Macclesfield

Peak District
National Park

LIURPOOL

● Coffee shops

15 Crosby Coffee – Oxford Road
16 The Sea Shanty
17 Bean Coffee Roasters – Liverpool One
18 Hardware Coffee + Kitchen
19 Bold Street Coffee – Liverpool
20 Crosby Coffee – Lark Lane
21 Press Bros Coffee
22 Bean There Coffee Shop
23 One Percent Forest

● Roasteries

50 Neighbourhood Coffee
51 Crosby Coffee Roasters

Locations are approximate

Waterloo
15

Seaforth

New Brighton
16

Wallasey

Bootle

50

51 Vauxhall

Liverpool City Centre

17 **18**

19

Wavertree

Birkenhead

Sefton Park

21

St Michael's Hamlet

20

22

Belle Vale

Mossley Hill

Woolton

23

River Mersey

MANCHESTER

● Coffee shops

34 Procaffeinated
35 Bold Street Coffee – Spinningfields
36 Federal – Deansgate
37 Atrium Coffee
38 Just Natas
39 Federal – Northern Quarter
40 Hampton & Voúis
41 SEESAW
42 Federal – Oxford Road

● Roasteries

55 Django Coffee Co.

Locations are approximate

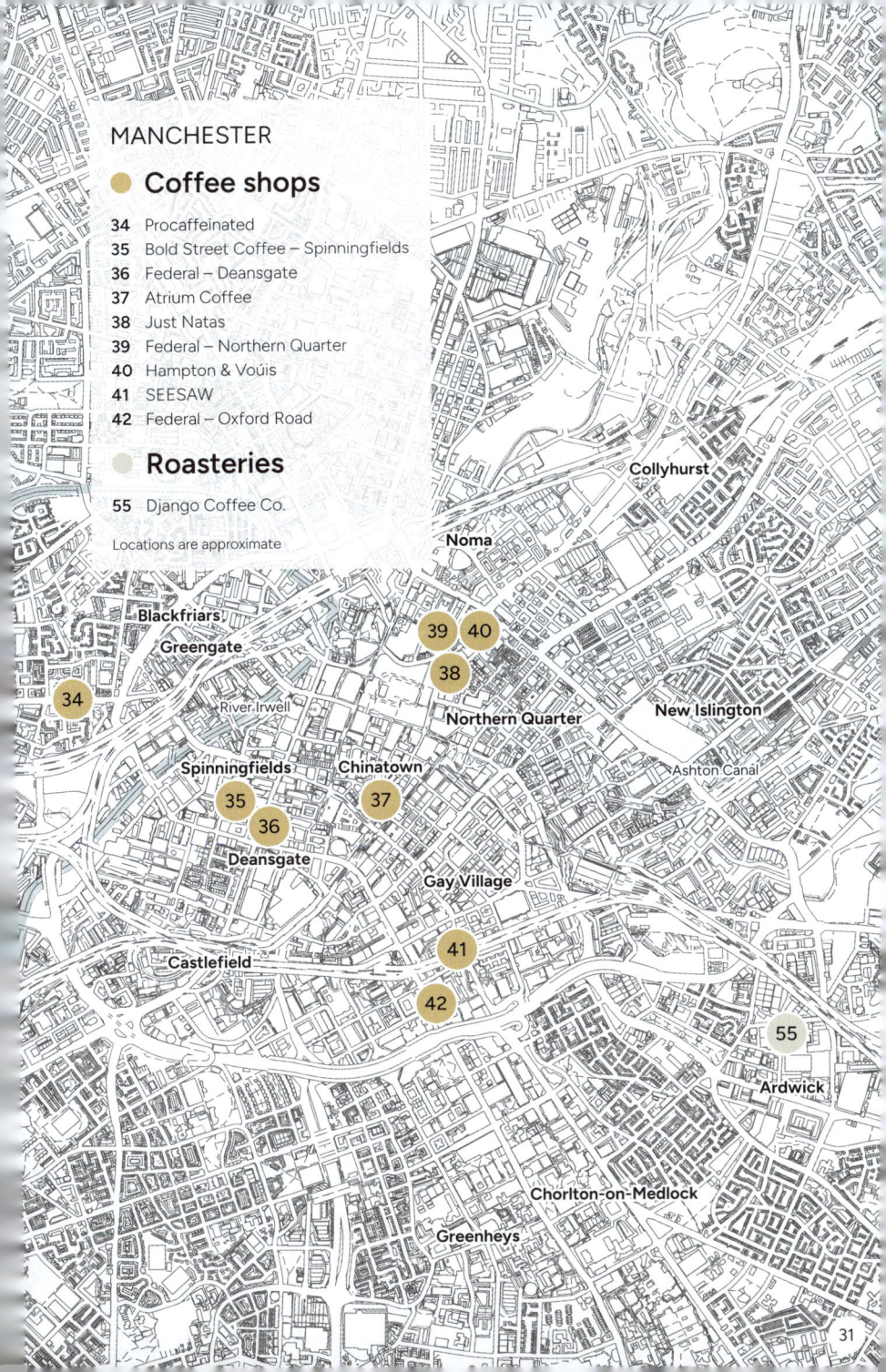

Collyhurst

Noma

Blackfriars

Greengate

34

River Irwell

39 40

38

Northern Quarter

New Islington

Ashton Canal

Spinningfields

Chinatown

35

37

36

Deansgate

Gay Village

Castlefield

41

42

55

Ardwick

Chorlton-on-Medlock

Greenheys

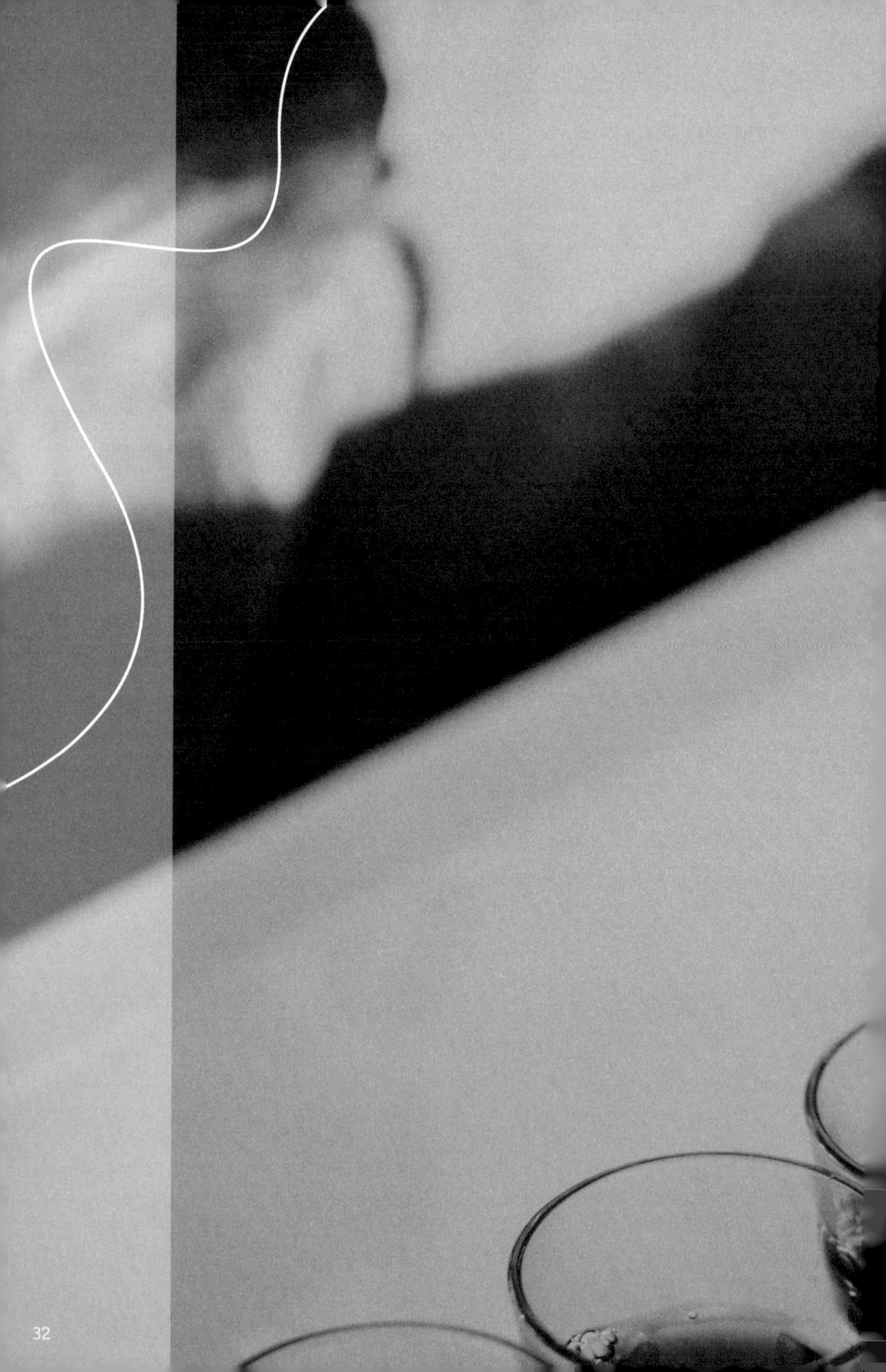

AREA 1
COFFEE SHOPS

46 Branthwaite Brow, Kendal, Cumbria, LA9 4TX

marra46.co.uk | 01539 731282

[O] marra46_kendal

BEEN THERE · BEEN THERE · BEEN THERE · BEEN THERE ·

Before he opened this cosy nook in the heart of Kendal, Marra founder James Tucker ran Yard 46, a popular cafe famed for its homemade small-batch sourdough. His next project was a street-food van which, following a win at the Cumbria Food Awards 2022, evolved into this bricks-and-mortar cafe and restaurant.

To find Marra's historical home from Branthwaite Brow, follow the swing sign down a narrow alley to a cobbled courtyard. Inside, blackened beams (rumoured to be from tall ships that were docked in Cumbria), a log burner and period features make it a snug spot in which to hunker down.

🛈 Check out sister cafe Crumb at Blackhall Yard for sourdough toasties to-go

Huddersfield roastery Dark Woods supplies the coffee, its Under Milk Wood blend (notes of caramel, praline and stewed fruits) used for espresso while Good Morning Sunshine (stone fruits, cocoa and cinder-toffee flavours) delivers on batch brew.

If you're out and about on a coffee tour, bookmark Marra for a lunch stop. The star of the show is the piadina (a twist on Italian street-food-style sarnies), but you'll also find sourdough pizza and flatbreads. If sweeter sustenance is needed, try one of the luscious cakes or a pastel de nata.

Established
2022

Key roastery
Dark Woods Coffee

Brewing method
Espresso, filter

Machine
Conti CC202

Grinder
Compak E6,
Bunn FPG,
Heycafe H1

Opening hours
Mon-Sat
10am-3pm

Kendal

Comida [food]

90-92 Highgate, Kendal, Cumbria, LA9 4HE

comidafood.co.uk | 01539 732082

 comidakendal comida_kendal

Adventure and beautiful scenery are a given on any trip to the Lake District and Cumbria, but what many visitors are also thrilled to discover on their travels through this part of the world is a thriving coffee scene. One spot stoking the speciality fire is Kendal's Comida [food] – a Med-inspired cafe and restaurant dealing in exceptional coffee and authentic tapas.

In combining their mutual passions for good food and coffee, Yorkshireman Simon Perkin and Spaniard Alba Basterra have created a relaxed destination where customers can fuel up on brunch and tapas dishes influenced by Alba's heritage, and speciality coffee bronzed by nearby roastery Red Bank.

☕ Embrace Spanish coffee culture with a Café Bombón

The silky house espresso makes a mean pairing with the cafe's brunch dishes. Choose from the likes of sobrasada, manchego and poached eggs on sourdough, topped tortillas, or the full 'spanglish' (bacon, eggs and mushrooms with chorizo, morcilla, paprika beans and patatas bravas). But leave a little room for a slice of burnt basque cheesecake paired with a delicately sweet filter brew.

From 12pm till late, tapas dishes such as boquerones, albondigas and salt-cod fritters come out to play alongside a considered selection of wines. Pop next door to sister pub 98 Highgate for a second bite of the Comida cherry.

Established
2017

Key roastery
Red Bank
Coffee Roasters

Brewing method
Espresso, filter

Machine
Sanremo Verona

Grinder
Victoria Arduino
Mythos One

Opening hours
Wed-Fri
12pm-10pm
Sat-Sun
10am-10pm

Kendal

(3) 98 Highgate

98 Highgate, Kendal, Cumbria, LA9 4HE

98highgate.co.uk | 01539 732082

 98highgate 98_highgate

BEEN THERE · BEEN THERE · BEEN THERE · BEEN THERE ·

Few bars manage to be at the heart of a town's social life quite as impressively as 98 Highgate. It's the kind of place where memories are made over coffee and cake, friendships forged over plates of tapas and plans hatched while sinking a local ale or two.

The plethora of events held in the space includes coffee mornings, Wonderful Wild Women drink and draw nights, singer-songwriter evenings, and DJ nights including Land of the Lost's Lost Afternoons and North Fire Sound's Catch-a-Vibe. For locals, it's not just a place to enjoy delicious espresso or filter brews crafted with beans roasted down the road by Red Bank, but also a meeting place, a laptop-friendly workspace and a sociable hub where they can enjoy a spot of speed quizzing.

Check out the local artists' exhibitions which appear regularly

Tapas and pub grub are delivered straight from its Spanish restaurant, Comida [food], next door. Hearty options like the Full Spanglish (chorizo, bacon, patatas bravas, morcilla, fried egg and mushrooms) jostle for attention with tapas dishes such as vegan albondigas (chickpea balls in tomato sauce).

The sweet-toothed shouldn't leave without getting their chops around the churros with chocolate – a wicked combo of fried dough, cinnamon sugar and dipping chocolate.

Established
2021

Key roastery
Red Bank
Coffee Roasters

Brewing method
Espresso, filter

Machine
La Marzocco
Linea Classic

Grinder
Victoria Arduino
Mythos One

Opening hours
Tue-Fri
9.30am-11pm
Sat
12pm-11pm

Kendal

36

Homeground Coffee + Kitchen

4 Homeground Coffee + Kitchen

This is a much-loved fave with both locals and the horde of visitors who flock to the Lake District each year. Rumour has it they go for the picturesque scenery but Homeground's creative menus and on-point pours may well be the real reason.

Main Road, Windemere, Cumbria, LA23 1DX

homegroundcafe.co.uk homegroundcafe

5 Fold

Fold yourself into a chair by the log burner and feed your appetite for beautifully crafted brews and stonking lunch and brunch dishes. While you're there, pick up interesting coffee and lifestyle gear and book onto one of the creative workshops.

Unit 12 Beezon Road Industrial Estate, Kendal, Cumbria, LA9 6BW

 fold_coffee

6 Atkinsons The Hall

Visit Atkinsons Coffee Roasters' OG cafe to taste the freshest coffees (bronzed next door) and chow down on quality carbs from its on-site bakery. Make sure you include a visit to its retail shop, a couple of doors down, which is crammed with beans, teas and brew kit.

10 China Street, Lancaster, Lancashire, LA1 1EX

thecoffeehopper.com atkinsons.coffee

Atkinsons The Hall

(7) Atkinsons The Castle

Lancaster Castle, Castle Hill, Lancaster, Lancashire, LA1 1YN

thecoffeehopper.com | 01524 65470

 lancastercastlecafe atkinsons.coffee

Generally, tourist attractions don't have a reputation for serving quality coffee, yet the restored Lancaster Castle bucks the trend and draws crowds for both its Norman architecture and single-origin espresso.

Overlooking the city for almost 1,000 years, the castle was a fully functioning prison until 2011. In 2019, after extensive renovation, it was opened to the public and the cafe in the grounds was entrusted to local speciality legends Atkinsons Coffee Roasters.

🔵 Don't leave town without visiting sister venues The Hall and The Music Room

The contemporary cafe is kitted out with birch plywood, metro tiles and houseplants, creating a modern counterpart to the historic setting. Take a seat on the piazza to enjoy an own-roasted flat white and freshly baked pastry while admiring the newly uncovered cloisters and restored turrets.

All the coffee beans, loose-leaf teas and baked goods are delivered daily from the Atkinsons roastery and bakery on China Street. The cafe's skilled baristas are happy to talk guests through the caffeinated options (these change almost daily) and recommend the best prep methods and flavour pairings.

Established
2019

Key roastery
Atkinsons
Coffee Roasters

Brewing method
Espresso, V60,
batch brew

Machine
Victoria Arduino
Eagle One

Grinder
Mahlkonig E65S

Opening hours
Mon-Sun
10am-4.45pm

Lancaster

(8) Journey Social

28 New Street, Lancaster, Lancashire, LA1 1EG

journeysocial.co.uk | 07561 550255

Journey Social Espresso Bar journeysociallancaster

Insta-worthy latte art, runny yolks, perfect french toast and fresh-from-the-oven bakes make this award-winning Lancaster hideout a big hitter when it comes to coffee and all-day dining.

Open every day of the week for banging brunches (served at all times of the day), it's little wonder there can be occasional competition for seats. However, queuing is no biggie when you know there's a brunch dish like the carrot-cake frenchie with your name on it. We're talking brioche loaf and warm carrot cake topped with carrot crisps, maple walnuts, hazelnut brittle and dried blood orange, doused with a scoop of crème fraîche and a splash of carrot sabayon.

Journey Social's all-day brunch isn't to be missed

The coffee shop's bake game is equally on point and the likes of blackberry and elderflower waffles vie for attention with sumptuous cinny buns and Rolo-topped brownies.

The high-calibre foodie experience requires an above-par drinks menu and Journey Social doesn't falter on that score. The speciality coffee line-up is headlined by London's Allpress Espresso, while guest roasts are available as V60.

Keep an eye out on socials for monthly pop-up evenings from the award-winning chefs. The elegant minimalist interior creates an irresistibly Instagrammable backdrop for the likes of taco feast nights.

Established
2018

Key roastery
Allpress Espresso

Brewing method
Espresso, V60, batch brew, Moccamaster

Machine
La Marzocco Linea PB

Grinder
Victoria Arduino Mythos One, Mahlkonig EK43

Opening hours
Mon-Sat
9am-5pm
Sun
9.30am-4pm

Lancaster

39

⑨ Rise – Preston

15 Miller Arcade, Preston, Lancashire, PR1 2QY

risebrunch.co.uk

🄾 risebrunch

Way more than just another brunch gaff, this buzzy Preston cafe takes the breakfast-to-lunch affair next level. It's a place to slow down, de-stress and reconnect with your favourite people while feasting on delicious dishes.

Inspired by antipodean cafes, Rise is light, bright and designed around a mix of intimate tables indoors and a sun-trap outdoors, making it a good find for all manner of social occasions. The menu – which includes added weekly specials and Insta-ready delights such as breakfast rolls, turkish eggs and açai bowls – also draws influence from down under.

☕ Share a side of potato hash which comes with pesto, parmesan and roast-garlic mayo

The coffee bolstering this brunch menu is sourced from pioneering roastery Ozone and prepared in a range of espresso drinks, with the addition of cold brew in the warmer months. Service is slick yet friendly and guests are encouraged to kick back and relax while the baristas get to work.

There's sometimes a queue (especially on Saturdays and Sundays, when weekend specials make the brunch bill especially enticing) but the wait is usually brief and always worth your time.

Established
2019

Key roastery
Ozone Coffee
Roasters

Brewing method
Espresso

Machine
La Marzocco Linea PB

Grinder
Mahlkonig E65S

Opening hours
Mon-Fri
8am-5pm
Sat-Sun
9am-5pm

Preston

Cedarwood Coffee Co.

10 Winckley Street, Preston, Lancashire, PR1 2AA

cedarwood.coffee | 03333 034352

cedarwoodcoffee cedarwoodcoffee

Preston's ever-popular coffee hangout can be found just beyond the Georgian splendour of Winckley Square. Visit for a decent brew, neighbourhood vibes, swift service and to watch the team keeping the community firing on all cylinders via pro serves and a heaving counter of sweet treats.

While B Corp-certified Dark Woods is the cafe's main roastery, Cedarwood dials up the ethical creds further by utilising beans from Red Bank Coffee Roasters, which uses a carefully sourced network of coffee producers. The beans from both roasteries are as sumptuously tasty as they are sustainably sound.

Grab a cortado to-go and take it on a walk through Winckley Square

Want to go off-piste with your drinks order? Choose between three affogato serves, dive into the strawberry oat matcha or check out the beer selection. Once you've plumped for your pick, savour it at a window seat or (when the weather's good) on the outdoor seating. Head to the upstairs area if you need a quiet space to power up the laptop and knuckle down or to cosy up with a good book.

The cafe enjoys a rep for killer cakes and cookies, so the eye-popping bakes are not to be missed. Toffee-apple blondies and cookies-and-cream brownies are always a hit or, for a double caffeine boost, pair your pourover with an espresso-caramel brownie.

Established
2015

Key roastery
Dark Woods Coffee

Brewing method
Espresso, V60

Machine
Sanremo Verona RS

Grinder
Sanremo SR70

Opening hours
Tue-Sat
10am-4.30pm
Sun
11am-4pm

Preston

41

Four1Two

412 Blackburn Road, Higher Wheelton, Chorley, Lancashire, PR6 8HX

four1two.com | 01254 433500

 fouronetwocafe four.1.two

BEEN THERE • BEEN THERE • BEEN THERE • BEEN THERE •

Sip a silky flat white, munch on a slice of something sweet, browse unusual gifts or even pick up flowers at this fusion venue in Higher Wheelton.

Four1Two is a collaboration between two families: coffee-and-bakes aficionados Scott and Bex run the cafe while Sophie manages the florist and gift shop.

Scott and Bex have recently switched up the cafe's house espresso offering to Langhūs, crafted by Holmfirth's Danelaw. The darker-roasted milk choc, toffee and raisin blend of Latin American beans is bold enough to stand up to milk yet sweet enough to create a cracking espresso. Whatever you choose, it would be ludicrous not to pair a brew with one of Bex's handcrafted bakes – try the triple chocolate brownie or one of the seasonally changing loaf cakes.

☕ Dog-friendly Four1Two is located near heaps of great trails for post-brunch walkies

The eats extend to an all-day savoury menu of cooked breakfasts, brunches and lunches, with everything made in-house and from scratch wherever possible (and sourced from local suppliers wherever not). Pray they have one of the seasonal french toast specials on the menu when you visit.

Don't leave without checking out the retail shelves of local artisan food and drink products, and picking up a bunch of blooms to take the good vibes home with you.

Established
2022

Key roastery
Danelaw Coffee

Brewing method
Espresso, pourover

Machine
Conti CC100

Grinder
Mazzer Kony

Opening hours
Mon, Wed-Fri
8am-4pm
Sat
9am-4pm
Sun
10am-3pm
(seasonal opening hours)

Chorley

(12) Siphon

91 Bank Street, Rawtenstall, Rossendale, Lancashire, BB4 7QN

siphonespresso.com

 siphonespressobrewbar siphonespresso

There aren't many places in Lancashire where you can score coffee prepared via syphon (or siphon) so if you're yet to watch the hypnotic prep method, it's worth making a trip to this cafe named in its honour.

The mesmerising method is just one of a range of brewing techniques employed at this specialist coffee bar. Espresso is, naturally, the most popular option, but founder Scott Moore also offers pourovers and cold brew.

⚡ Sound the klaxon! A new Siphon coffee shop will open in 2025

The coffee menu revolves around roasts from Crosby Coffee in Liverpool, and is headlined by the roastery's Iron Men blend which delivers a mean flat white with notes of dark choc and hazelnut. Bringing a coffee-averse chum? They'll be delighted with the range from Brew Tea Co.

There's also an impressive selection of freshly baked pastries, cookies and homemade bakes, which makes popping in for just a coffee nigh-on impossible. A small menu of staple dishes (think bacon, spinach and cream cheese on sourdough, and homemade banana bread with mascarpone and blueberries) offers heartier options for breakfast and lunchtime visits.

Established
2018

Key roastery
Crosby Coffee

Brewing method
Espresso, pourover, syphon, cold brew

Machine
Sanremo Verona RS

Grinder
Eureka Mythos

Opening hours
Mon-Thu
8.30am-3pm
Fri-Sat
8.30am-4pm
Sun
10am-3pm

Rawtenstall

43

13 Two Brothers – Ormskirk

Ormskirk Food and Drink Market, Moorgate, Ormskirk, Lancashire, L39 4RT

twobrothers.coffee

f twobrotherscoffeeltd 🄾 twobrotherscoffee

With the hospitality industry facing ever-rising overheads, businesses have had to find increasingly inventive ways to deliver delicious food and drink to customers without stressing over how to keep the lights on.

In the historic market town of Ormskirk, six food traders, a bar and one pioneering coffee shop have teamed up to create the Ormskirk Food and Drink Market. This is a collective space where discerning customers can scoff good food, sip quality coffee, listen to live music and hang out with their mates.

⚫ Finesse your coffee-tasting game by signing up for a cupping session

The creative set-up gives Two Brothers the peculiar honour of being, simultaneously, both the smallest and biggest speciality coffee shop in Ormskirk. This is because, while they have a handful of tables in their street-front shop, they also serve customers in the 300-seat market space through a hatch in the wall.

The majority of the coffee is roasted in-house by the Two Brothers team at a sister shop in Warrington, 18 miles away. As a result, there are always fresh and exciting beans from different origins to explore, as well as a selection of loose-leaf teas, indulgent hot chocolates and fresh-from-the-oven treats.

Established
2023

Key roastery
Two Brothers

Brewing method
Espresso, batch brew, V60, Clever Dripper

Machine
La Marzocco FB80

Grinder
Victoria Arduino Mythos One, Mahlkonig EK43

Opening hours
Mon-Fri
7am-5pm
Sat
8am-6pm
Sun
8.30am-4pm

Ormskirk

44

14 Crosby Coffee – Hightown

2 Alt Road, Hightown, Liverpool, Merseyside, L38 0BF

crosbycoffee.co.uk

crosbycoffeeltd crosbycoffeeltd

© Daniel Piercy

BEEN THERE · BEEN THERE · BEEN THERE ·

The juggernaut – well, maybe babynaut, as it's still very artisan – that is Crosby Coffee keeps on coming up with delicious offerings for the caffeine lovers of Liverpool. The latest example is this spanking new third site.

The coffee shop offers something a little different from its siblings in that customers can choose their preferred profile of filter coffee – fruity, nutty and so on – before selecting the brew method they'd like used to coax out the nuanced flavours. The baristas are super friendly and love to engage in coffee chat, so feel free to quiz them on the menu, methods and stories behind the beans. Beans, kit and accessories are stocked so visitors can pick up the gear to try and recreate the Crosby coffee experience at home.

🔆 Don't leave without trying one of the whopping cheese and prosciutto croissants

In conjunction with this launch, the team have started to collaborate with local bakeries Solobread and Pastille Bakery. They're not the only local suppliers the cafe likes to support: syrups are sourced from William Fox, matcha powder from Pink Panda and chocolates through Table Chocolate.

Cyclists and four-legged friends are welcomed and well catered for.

Established
2024

Key roastery
Crosby Coffee Roasters

Brewing method
Espresso, Chemex, V60, AeroPress, batch brew

Machine
Conti MC Ultima

Grinder
Compak E8 DBW, Compak E6 x2, Mahlkonig EK43

Opening hours
Mon-Fri
8am-5pm
Sat-Sun
9am-4pm

Liverpool

45

Flip
Your Lid

New Commuter Travel Mug.
Fully sealed flip lid, insulated,
90% recycled stainless steel.

keepcup.com

Crosby Coffee – Oxford Road

2 Oxford Road, Waterloo, Liverpool, Merseyside, L22 8QF

crosbycoffee.co.uk

crosbycoffeeltd crosbycoffeeltd

BEEN THERE · BEEN THERE · BEEN THERE · BEEN THERE

Crosby Coffee is something of a community hub in Waterloo, hosting friends catching up over flat whites and croissants, remote workers escaping the home office, and new mums craving caffeinated respite.

With a food menu built around carby goods from a local sourdough bakery, and a basement seating area lined with benches and plenty of plug sockets to keep laptops powered, the whole experience maxes out customer satisfaction.

⚡ Sneak off to the downstairs snug – complete with lamps and comfy couches – for a chilled vibe

However, Crosby's ultimate selling point is its coffee, which is roasted in-house using sustainably sourced beans from Africa and South America. There are three grinders for espresso alone, and with the flavour-bomb beans rotated each week there's always something new to try. Pourover purists will be stoked to explore the new filter offering: choose between fruity, floral or nutty profiles before selecting from a range of brewing methods including V60, Kalita Wave and Chemex.

All of the beans at the bar are available in retail packs to take home or can be delivered direct through the roastery's monthly subscription service.

Established
2017

Key roastery
Crosby Coffee
Roasters

Brewing method
Espresso, batch brew,
V60, Kalita Wave,
Chemex, AeroPress

Machine
Conti Monte
Carlo Ultima

Grinder
Compak E8 DBW,
Compak E6,
Mahlkonig EK43

Opening hours
Mon-Fri
8am-5pm
Sat-Sun
9am-4pm

Liverpool

48

4 Atherton Street, New Brighton, Merseyside, CH45 2NY

07342 018207

f theseashantynewbrighton [ig] theseashanty

What shall we do with the drunken sailor? Haul him down to New Brighton's The Sea Shanty for speciality coffee and community vibes.

It's a home-from-home for many. Regulars are known by name because the Shanty is where they get together to play live music at the Shanty Sessions on the first and last Friday of the month at midday, meet for chess club (every Thursday 11am-1pm), or buy a coffee for someone who needs cheering up via the coffee-for-a-stranger scheme. There are even recycled litter pickers available for those who want to do a beach clean.

⚡ Sunny day? Take your brew to the urban patio garden to soak up the rays as you sip

Fuelling the community feels is a top-notch house espresso – a medium-roast washed Colombian with notes of caramel, cocoa and walnut – from Wirral's Adams + Russell. Or sample whichever guest filter is featured on V60 (it's switched up every couple of months).

Pair your brew with something sweet – cakes are baked in-house and mostly vegan and gluten-free – then sink into the chilled atmosphere of this friendly spot. Perch beside a window amid the houseplants and enjoy the great background tunes as you indulge.

Established
2018

Key roastery
Adams + Russell
Coffee Roasters

Brewing method
Espresso, V60

Machine
Expobar G10

Grinder
969 Noveseinove

Opening hours
Mon-Sun
10am-4pm

New Brighton

(17) **Bean Coffee Roasters** – **Liverpool One**

18-20 College Lane, Liverpool, Merseyside, L1 3DS

beancoffee.co.uk | 01513 759721

f beancoffeeuk beancoffeeuk

Whether you're just starting out on your speciality coffee journey or are a self-confessed bean fanatic, you'll discover new coffees to light up your palate at this happening hub in the heart of Liverpool's shopping district.

The friendly team of baristas are dedicated to crafting exceptional coffee which has been roasted in their Loring roaster at nearby Brunswick Dock. The house coffee, Bean Blend, is a chocolatey and red-berry-forward combination of Brazilian, Nicaraguan and Indian beans, and backed up by a selection of single origins.

Thirsty for more? Check out the brewing courses

For a more immersive coffee-tasting experience, position yourself at the brew bar where the baristas can guide you through a drinks menu dictated by flavour. Experiment with new notes and brewing techniques, then pick up some beans and coffee gear to relive the flavour odyssey at home.

One of 18 Bean Coffee outposts across the country, this particular coffee shop is in an ideal location for refuelling after a spot of retail therapy. Whichever brew you end up slurping, freshly made sandwiches and cinny buns make a replenishing accompaniment to your preferred pour.

Established
2021

Key roastery
Bean Coffee Roasters

Brewing method
Espresso, V60,
Chemex, AeroPress,
3TEMP batch brew

Machine
Victoria Arduino
Black Eagle Maverick,
Modbar

Grinder
Mahlkonig E65S x2,
Mahlkonig EK43,
Mahlkonig E80

Opening hours
Mon-Sat
7.30am-8pm
Sun
9am-6pm

Liverpool

Hardware Coffee + Kitchen

40b Renshaw Street, Liverpool, Merseyside, L1 4EF

hardwareliverpool.co.uk

Hardware Coffee + Kitchen hardware_liverpool

Hardware Coffee + Kitchen, known fondly as Hardy's, draws its name and character from the building's former life as a hardware store. This history is reflected in the exposed brick walls, hardwood floors and assortment of tools displayed on the walls. The result is a grounded-yet-contemporary space in which to imbibe quality coffee and tuck into cafe fodder.

A recently refreshed brunch menu strikes a balance between familiar and inventive. Dishes like the Brekkie Burger (sausage patty, bacon, gouda, hash brown and a fried egg in a toasted brioche bun) slide up next to pistachio french toast – a spin on a brunch classic which comes laden with pistachio mascarpone, lemon curd, berry coulis, lemon zest and pistachio crumb. And with seasonal specials introduced every two weeks, there's always something new to discover.

Celebrating? Swap your coffee order for one of the creative cocktails

Hardy's collaborates with Liverpool's Neighbourhood Coffee to ensure the house 'spros are always bang-on. A rotation of guest espresso beans from roasteries like Blossom and ALL CAPS provide further thrills. Meanwhile, playful drink specials alternate every fortnight – previous seasonal creations have included dragon fruit coconut matcha and Biscoff latte.

Established
2022

Key roastery
Neighbourhood Coffee

Brewing method
Espresso, drip, cold brew

Machine
La Marzocco Linea PB

Grinder
Mahlkonig E80S, Anfim Pratica

Opening hours
Mon-Sun
7am-5pm

Liverpool

Bold Street Coffee – Liverpool

89 Bold Street, Liverpool, Merseyside, L1 4HF

boldstreetcoffee.co.uk

bold.streetcoffee boldstreetcoffee

All hail the original Bold Street Coffee, a bustling spot that's been churning out speciality coffee and top-notch brunches all day every day for nearly 15 years.

The award-winning cafe is loved for its own-roasted coffee, selection of guest roasts and brunch options – the signature 'buoys' being almost as enticing as the range of brews. For those unfamiliar, buoys are toasted brioche buns filled with scrambled eggs and melted cheese, which can be pimped to include sausage, bacon and hash browns. A stellar vegan buoy is also available.

The iced drinks are next level. Or cool down with a coffee soft-serve

As well as roasting their own beans in the city (sample them here and in the other five BSC cafes across Liverpool and Manchester), the Bold Street massive also showcase the roasting talents of Origo, The Barn, Sumo, Newground, Red Bank and Fort.

The house coffee, however, is the star serve and allows the team to deliver up the freshest beans, which have been crafted with skill and care. If you like what you taste, buy a bag of beans in store to-go, or order online for delivery to home. A subscription service for espresso, filter and decaf coffees is also available.

Established
2010

Key roastery
Bold Street Coffee

Brewing method
Espresso, batch brew

Machine
Conti Monte
Carlo Ultima

Grinder
Compak E8,
Compak Bolt 83

Opening hours
Mon-Sat
8am-6pm
Sun
9am-5pm

Liverpool

⟨20⟩ Crosby Coffee – Lark Lane

62 Lark Lane, Aigburth, Liverpool, Merseyside, L17 8UP

crosbycoffee.co.uk

🅕 crosbycoffeeltd 🅞 crosbycoffeeltd

The middle child in the Crosby family of coffee shops, this outpost is found in the leafy Liverpool suburb of Aigburth. The team have made the most of the narrow venue, cleverly positioning tables and adding seating to the snug basement to create a functional and welcoming cafe space.

As you'd expect at a Crosby venue, the star attraction is the speciality coffee – as well as the people who serve it. The baristas are delighted to share their own coffee recipes with regulars, and some even hold lofty titles like Barista of the Year from the Liverpool Hospitality People Awards.

🔵 Get involved in one of the regular community events

All the beans are roasted at Crosby HQ's new spot on Glegg Street. They arrive fresh and fragrant, and are fed into the hoppers of three grinders to give discerning drinkers a choice of single origins and house blends.

Those looking to brush up their own barista skills can pick up beans, kit and accessories from the retail shelves. A refreshed food menu is another reason to visit; simple brunches made with quality local ingredients add another authentic feather to the cap of this bustling coffee shop.

Established
2021

Key roastery
Crosby Coffee Roasters

Brewing method
Espresso,
Clever Dripper, V60,
AeroPress, batch brew

Machine
Conti Monte
Carlo Ultima

Grinder
Compak E8 DBW,
Compak E6,
Mahlkonig EK43

Opening hours
Mon-Fri
8am-5pm
Sat-Sun
9am-4pm

Liverpool

53

Press Bros Coffee

82 Lark Lane, Liverpool, Merseyside, L17 8UU

pressbroscoffee.co.uk

pressbroscoffee

In need of a caffeine hit, a social pick-me-up or comforting scran? Lean into the brotherly love and cheerful caffeination to be found at bros Oli and Tito Press's Lark Lane cafe.

The pair started their coffee careers in 2017, serving brews from a converted Piaggio van in the Baltic Market. Then, after four years, they moved to this bricks-and-mortar site. Sandwiched between other indies in a bohemian location, the vibrant cafe is a great spot for diving into an extensive range of speciality coffees from some of the UK's best roasteries.

🍩 Every day is cinny bun day at Press Bros – the housemade buns are *chef's kiss*

Beans are supplied by the likes of Neighbourhood, Rascal, Harmony, Extract and, more recently, Press Bros. The brothers dropped a beany bombshell with the release of Dulima – their washed Colombian showcasing notes of chocolate, caramel and red berries – and have further roasting plans up their sleeves.

Thankfully, there are enough hoppers to keep up with the influx of fresh beans. Two house espressos (usually a fruity Ethiopian and a chocolatey Brazilian or Colombian) are available alongside a guest 'spro, while a fourth grinder is reserved for own-roasted decaf. Two funky filter specials also feature.

Pair your pick of the drinks menu with edibles like sarnies, patty melts and french toast.

Established
2021

Key roastery
Multiple roasteries

Brewing method
Espresso, AeroPress, V60, drip

Machine
La Marzocco KB90

Grinder
Mahlkonig EK43, Mahlkonig E80 x 2, Anfim Pratica x 2

Opening hours
Mon-Sun
8.30am-5pm

Liverpool

54

22 Bean There Coffee Shop

376 Smithdown Road, Wavertree, Liverpool, Merseyside, L15 5AN
beantherecoffeeshop.com | 01513 093046

f beantherecoffeeshop beantherecoffeeshop

Those stopping by Bean There's coffee shop to grab a sourdough loaf, sarnie, sausage roll, hunk of cake or afternoon tea (a new addition to the menu) will enjoy knowing every element was freshly made from scratch that morning at the Bean There bakery on Rose Lane.

☀ Sunny day? Take a pew on the new outdoor garden seating in Penny Lane

The bakes at this friendly neighbourhood cafe are equalled only by its champion coffee offering. Alongside the espresso house beans from Lancaster's roasting heavyweight Atkinsons are single-origin offerings courtesy of a carousel of UK roasteries. Recent highlights include Edinburgh's Machina, Coleraine's Fidela and Liverpool's West Coast and Neighbourhood. Sample them as batch, V60 or Chemex, paired with high quality (and sustainable) local milk from Peckforton Farm Dairy.

The Bean There feast for the senses is heightened by regular community activities such as art exhibitions and craft workshops — keep an eye on socials for upcoming events.

Bringing a crowd for brekkie? The gang serve a whopping croissant designed to feed ten people.

Established
2017

Key roastery
Atkinsons Coffee Roasters

Brewing method
Espresso, batch brew, Chemex, V60

Machine
La Marzocco Linea PB, Victoria Arduino Eagle One

Grinder
Victoria Arduino Mythos One

Opening hours
Mon-Fri
8am-5pm
Sat-Sun
9am-5pm

Liverpool

(23) One Percent Forest

42 Allerton Road, Woolton, Liverpool, Merseyside, L25 7RG

onepercentforest.co.uk

 onepercentforest onepercentforest

Hej! In true Nordic style, this minimalist shop and bar is strong on community vibes, and was launched through a Kickstarter campaign by founders Dean Caffery and Hannah Sharp.

The locals who backed it have been handsomely rewarded with a cafe that not only channels a warm and cosy atmos but also a coffee menu featuring an exciting range of beans from Dark Woods, Assembly, Dark Arts, Round Hill and ALL CAPS. These beans are fashioned into espresso drinks and batch brew, as well as seasonal pours such as the house iced latte (served with a smidgen of agave and a twist of juicy orange). Then, as the sun goes down, Nordic-style cocktails are served up and the cafe seamlessly morphs into a hygge-cool bar.

Bookworm coffee geek?
You'll want to join the OPF book club

OPF, as it's known locally, aims for minimalism across the board, an ethos that extends to its menu of edibles. The team keep it simple, serving just a few core items at any one time in order to focus on doing a small number of things incredibly well.

Added extras include a furry wall of fame for local dogs who frequent the space, and an OPF loyalty app.

Established
2018

Key roastery
Dark Woods Coffee

Brewing method
Espresso, batch brew

Machine
La Marzocco Linea

Grinder
Victoria Arduino Mythos One

Opening hours
Mon-Thu
8.30am-4pm
Fri-Sat
8.30am-11pm
Sun
9am-5pm

Liverpool

⟨24⟩ **Two Brothers – Warrington**

Warrington Market, 2 Times Square, Warrington, Cheshire, WA1 2NT

twobrothers.coffee

f twobrotherscoffeeltd **◉** twobrotherscoffee

Despite its contemporary glass-fronted facade there's something wonderfully old school about Warrington Market, which is home to over 50 independent shops and food vendors.

Amid the lively buzz of market traders selling their wares, discover an oasis of calm and a first-rate brew at Two Brothers, where exceptional beans and a serene atmosphere provide a moment of respite.

Behind the sleek hardwood countertop, head roaster Natalie and coffee expert Sean operate the Giesen roaster and slurp from cupping spoons to create Two Brothers' beautifully balanced coffees. Peaberry beans are used to create the house espresso and offer a cornucopia of earthy flavours, including chocolate, berry and walnut. If you're unsure what to try, the team are happy to advise on the perfect pour to match your mood.

🔆 While coffee is the main draw, the matcha lattes are also pretty fine

A smattering of tables and chairs in the atrium in front of the coffee bar offers people-watching opportunities as you sip your brew. Round off the experience with a slab of vegan chocolate brownie or a slice of springy banana chocolate loaf.

Established
2020

Key roastery
Two Brothers

Brewing method
Espresso, batch brew, Clever Dripper, V60

Machine
La Marzocco FB80

Grinder
Victoria Arduino Mythos One, Victoria Arduino Mythos MY75, Mahlkonig EK43

Opening hours
Mon-Sat
9am-5pm
Sun
10am-4pm

Warrington

Bean & Cole

41 Frodsham Street, Chester, Cheshire, CH1 3JJ

beanandcole.co.uk

 beanandcole beanandcolecoffee

After spending a year in the exceptional coffee scene down under, founders Ian and Nicole were inspired to recreate the same kind of cosy-but-cool cafe back home in the UK. So now, in the heart of Chester, coffee lovers can experience warm and fuzzy neighbourhood vibes and quality brews at the Bean & Cole HQ (Ian's nickname is Bean, Cole comes from Nicole).

Hotfoot it to Bean & Cole's new site in Chester's New Market for more adventures in speciality coffee

Energising smoothie bowls star on the menu alongside a tempting selection of toasties and topped toast – regulars are often drawn to Bean & Cole's signature grilled cheese or spicy avocado toast. There are always new additions to the menu which keep the offering fresh, and include seasonal pastries and cakes from The Bear Bakery.

The house coffee accompanying the delicious fodder is sourced from PLOT, while a rotating roster of guest roasteries also features and includes Assembly, Round Hill, Three Marks and Cloud Picker.

Bean & Cole has made a name for itself locally for hosting roastery takeovers and cupping events, which always go down a storm thanks to its trademark chilled atmosphere and friendly team.

Established
2018

Key roastery
PLOT Roasting

Brewing method
Espresso, batch brew, V60

Machine
La Marzocco KB90 3AV, Victoria Arduino White Eagle 2AV

Grinder
Mahlkonig E65 GbW, Mahlkonig E80

Opening hours
Mon-Sat
9am-5pm
Sun
9am-4pm

Chester

Malt Street (in King Steet Car Park), Knutsford, Cheshire, WA16 6E

 tattonperk tattonperk

Tatton Perk is the passion project of former probation officer Mark Lee-Kilgariff who, in 2018, traded in the nine to five for a vintage Peugeot J7 van. His plan was to quietly serve cracking brews to parents in the local park while listening to jazz.

It didn't go exactly to plan: word spread, the coffee rep grew and within four years Mark had set up a bricks and mortar HQ in the park to satisfy ballooning demand.

Now, Tatton Perk is an all-important community hub and headed up by manager Mia who leads the crew behind the barista bar.

Move quickly to nab a coffee-glazed cinny bun – on weekends they go like hot cakes

Although most customers visit to grab 'n' go (many have muddy four-legged friends in tow after a jaunt in the park) the cosy cafe does have a smattering of seating, should you prefer to sit inside and savour a silky V60 pourover.

Most of the coffee beans used are Archetype from Lancaster's Atkinsons, which has proved to be a perennial fave with the locals. An ever-growing range of locally baked cakes is just as popular and includes saucer-sized eccles cakes and gigantic stuffed cookies.

Established
2022

Key roastery
Atkinsons Coffee Roasters

Brewing method
Espresso, V60

Machine
Sanremo Verona RS

Grinder
Mahlkonig E65S

Opening hours
Mon-Sat
8am-4pm
Sun
9am-4pm

Knutsford

Two Brothers – Altrincham

53 Stamford New Road, Altrincham, Cheshire, WA14 1DS

twobrothers.coffee

 twobrotherscoffeeltd twobrotherscoffee

Two Brothers in Altrincham is the siblings' founding coffee shop – offshoot outposts can be found in Warrington and Ormskirk.

The cafe's interior provides an insight into brothers Steve and Dave's previous careers as electrical engineers as it's got a sleek, industrial vibe. Exposed Edison bulbs dangle from the ceiling, casting a cosy glow over the wooden counter, tabletops and dark walls.

Despite a counter groaning with a glut of baked goods (including gluten-free and vegan options), the main draw is the coffee. Expertly own-roasted beans are showcased in a range of espresso drinks, pourovers and, more recently, Clever Dripper, assuring a caffeinated experience to suit every palate and mood. The coffees are rotated regularly, so there's always something new to try. And the attention to detail paid to the coffee is mirrored by excellent service from the barista team.

🡒 Pick up a bag of Two Brothers beans to continue the good sipping at home

Park yourself on a comfy leather chair with your brew and a fresh cinnamon roll or a slice of zingy lemon, pistachio and white chocolate cake and watch the world go by.

Established
2017

Key roastery
Two Brothers

Brewing method
Espresso, batch brew, Clever Dripper, V60

Machine
Sanremo Opera

Grinder
Victoria Arduino Mythos One x 2, Mahlkonig EK43

Opening hours
Mon-Fri
7am-5pm
Sat
8am-5pm
Sun
8.30am-4pm

Altrincham

Federal – Coffee Cart

Greenwood Street, Altrincham, Cheshire, WA14 1SA

federalcafe.co.uk | 01614 250974

f federalcafebar **⊙** federalcafebar

Chewy anzac biscuits and crema-rich espresso await visitors of this cute little coffee cart.

As expected from a Federal coffee spot, the drinks are always of superlative quality and the service efficient yet friendly. Each one of its coffee destinations channels Aussie cafe culture and the cart is no exception – if you don't know which sweet bake to pair with your brew, the crew are likely to recommend a Tim Tam.

💡 Bring your pooch along and the staff will make a fuss of them – no exceptions

The coffee cart launched during lockdown in Altrincham Market on specific market days but was so popular it's now open seven days a week. Locals appreciate how the staff know their order by heart, while newbies are always impressed by the calibre of the caffeine from such a small set-up (the Ozone-backed brews never disappoint). If you like what you swig, bags of beans are available to purchase.

For a sweeter pick-me-up or alternative to the usual espresso order, look no further than the hot Milo, matcha or chai. Drop into Federal's outposts in Deansgate, Northern Quarter and Oxford Road for a heartier feed or longer coffee break.

Established
2021

Key roastery
Ozone Coffee

Brewing method
Espresso

Machine
La Marzocco Linea PB

Grinder
Mythos One

Opening hours
Mon-Sun
8am-4pm

Altrincham

(29) Oscillate Coffee

52 Flixton Road, Urmston, Manchester, M41 5AB

oscillatecoffee.com

oscillatecoffee

In the centre of Urmston, Oscillate has quickly established itself as a serene sanctuary for bean geeks thanks to its bill of coffees hailing from various world-class roasteries.

The core line-up includes Blossom, Friedhats, Dak and A.M.O.C, while guest appearances from Sweven, People Possession, Kawa and Rose Coffee Roasters also feature. Swing by to discover unusual bean varietals and cutting-edge processing techniques.

The drinks menu is a celebration of coffees from different origins which are brewed with precision for espresso perfection. Hand brews are another highlight and skilfully prepped using the Orea V4 or Origami Drippers.

⚡ Limited-edition coffees are always on rotation — ask what's new

A minimalist Scandi-style interior of white walls, natural light and clean lines provides a calming backdrop in which to relish in-house bakes, freshly made sandwiches and a seasonally changing menu.

The relaxed atmosphere invites customers to linger while savouring every sip of artisanal coffee. This isn't just a coffee drop-in; it's a destination for the brew-obsessed.

Established
2023

Key roastery
Multiple roasteries

Brewing method
Espresso, Orea,
Origami Dripper

Machine
La Marzocco Linea PB

Grinder
Mahlkonig E65S,
Mahlkonig EK43,
Anfim Luna

Opening hours
Mon-Fri
8am-4pm
Sat
9am-4pm

Manchester

62

(30) SWIG

Brookburn Road, Chorlton, Greater Manchester, M21 9ES

07771 939569

[instagram] swigcoffeee

Coffee fiends in the Chorlton area of Manchester will have clocked the retro van from which barista and photographer Kai Giraulo Corneill takes enormous pride in crafting delicious espresso and serving locally baked cakes.

Kai is on a mission to ensure that even those who can't regularly get to a good coffee shop can still savour quality beans roasted by Macclesfield's Kickback and expertly pulled through his mobile Sanremo Zoe.

At his permanent spot on Brookburn Road, those in need of caffeinated refuelling can pair a flat white with a seasonal bake – Kai mixes up the offering but the likes of brownies, pastel de nata, almond croissants and sausage rolls have all featured.

⚡ Swerving coffee? Kai makes a mean matcha latte

'What makes SWIG (see where I go) unique is that we are serving high-quality speciality coffee from the back of a retro van around a cool and famous city like Manchester,' says Kai. 'With such a small space I aim to make customers happy by producing the best I possibly can.'

Posts on social reveal the locations, events and festivals where Kai and Betsy the Bedford rock up each day.

Established
2024

Key roastery
Kickback Coffee
Roasters

Brewing method
Espresso

Machine
Sanremo Zoe

Grinder
Eureka Zenith Neo

Opening hours
Tue-Thu
8am-3pm
Fri-Sun
9am-3pm

31 SMOAK

105 Manchester Road, Chorlton, Manchester, M21 9GA

smoak.coffee

[f] levyhomefood [◎] smoak.coffee

When the dream of opening his own cafe was scuppered on the eve of the Covid pandemic, Jonathan Barnett instead turned his attention to the art of smoking meat. Then, in 2022, he got the opportunity to combine his meat-smoking hobby with his passion for a good cup of joe and SMOAK was launched. Today, the waft of freshly roasted beans and the earthy tang of cured beef lure passersby into this cafe in Chorlton, where first-rate sips and fully loaded bagels combine in delicious harmony.

ⓥ Vegan? Check out the smoked organic tofu bagel

From curing salt beef to 'smoaking' harissa and aubergine puree, every element is crafted with care. The bagels, delivered fresh each morning, complement the house espresso blend from Heart and Graft, while guest single-origin coffees from niche roasteries bring variety to the menu.

Specialities on a standout brunch lineup include salt beef and smoked-tofu bagels. Or, for a taste of New York with a Chorlton twist, don't miss The Works: salt beef, emmental, poached eggs, kraut, pickles and mustard mayo. Halal-friendly and endlessly creative with its bagel fillings and homemade sauces, SMOAK has become the go-to lunch spot for locals in this part of town.

Established
2022

Key roastery
Heart and Graft
Coffee Roastery

Brewing method
Espresso, batch brew

Machine
Victoria Arduino
Eagle One

Grinder
Mahlkonig E65S GbW

Opening hours
Mon-Sun
8am-3.30pm

Chorlton

Hikari Koffee

41 Barlow Moor Road, Didsbury, Manchester, M20 6TW

07746 136283

BEEN THERE · BEEN THERE · BEEN THERE

f Hikari Koffee ⊙ hikarikoffee

This hole-in-the-wall coffee shop, tucked inside a barbershop, has brought speciality vibes with a Japanese twist to the leafy suburb of Didsbury.

The name Hikari translates as 'light' in Japanese — apt for a coffee kiosk whose purpose is to craft joy-inducing drinks. It's also the name of owner Terry Liu's gorgeous furball — an Akita pup — who features in the cafe's coffee-cup logo as well as doing sterling work greeting customers IRL.

🍃 Mix up your matcha order with a hojicha latte, made using roasted green tea

Terry trained as a barista in coffee shops in Hong Kong and utilises his pro skills delivering a variety of espresso and filter pours. There are always four different single-origin espresso picks to be found on the menu: a dark and nutty Brazilian house coffee roasted by Swan Song, and three rotating guest roasts that deliver chocolatey, fruity, floral or funky flavours.

For Japanese-inspired refreshment, check out the yuzu lemon iced tea (yuzu, honey, lemon and cold-brew green tea), the Sunrise iced coffee (a blend of espresso, tonic and yuzu honey) or the Sunset iced brew (espresso, tonic and grapefruit juice).

Established
2024

Key roastery
Swan Song Coffee

Brewing method
Espresso, batch brew, pourover

Machine
Decent DE1,
La Marzocco
Linea Mini

Grinder
Mahlkonig E65S,
Lagom P64,
Mazzer Philos

Opening hours
Tue-Fri
7.30am-3pm
Sat
9am-4pm
Sun
9.30am-4pm

Didsbury

Something More Productive

9 Egerton Crescent, Withington, Greater Manchester, M20 4PN

somethingmoreproductive

© Andy Frost

What happens when you combine a passion for speciality coffee with a love of quality food and jazz? Something More Productive, that's what.

Since opening in 2023, the cafe has become a beacon in its community, thanks to the welcoming approach of owner Theo Tobias and his crew — which includes key team member Roscoe the cockapoo.

Their small-batch coffee offering keeps brew geeks on their toes as the house espresso is switched up every few months — or whenever local roastery Kobean secures a limited lot that can be exclusive to SMP. For decaf and a daily rotating filter selection, Swan Song provides the goods. Beans from both roasteries adorn the retail shelves, so visitors can pick up coffee beans to-go. Whichever brew you plump for, enjoy sipping it from a gorgeously handcrafted mug made by a local ceramicist.

⚡ SMP share their skills at weekly barista training sessions

On the food front, the crew eschew standard brunch fare in favour of creative seasonal sarnies such as korean barbecue bành-mí with gochujang mushrooms, vegan mayo, carrot and cabbage slaw, spring onions and black sesame seeds.

From Thursday to Saturday, an evening service sees the laid-back cafe vibes morph into a groovy jazz-club atmosphere. Find the team slinging homemade pizzas paired with wine, cocktails, local beers on tap and a whole load of bebop.

Established
2023

Key roastery
Kobean Coffee Roasters

Brewing method
Espresso, filter, V60

Machine
Victoria Arduino Eagle One

Grinder
Mahlkonig E65S, Mahlkonig EK43

Opening hours
Mon-Wed
8am-4pm
Thu-Sat
8am-10.30pm
Sun
9am-4pm

Withington

Procaffeinated

263 Chapel Street, Salford, Greater Manchester, M3 5JY

procaffeinatedmcr procaffeinatedmcr

Procaffeinated owners Daniel Haralambous and Ilaria Criscuolo fell for each other – and speciality coffee – when working together in the Amsterdam coffee scene. The couple returned to the UK and embedded themselves in Manchester's thriving speciality sector before launching their own venture in Salford.

The cafe brings chilled and earthy vibes to Chapel Street, thanks to its vaulted ceiling trailing with greenery, huge windows that flood the building with light, and custom-made steel and reclaimed-wood furniture which injects warmth into the industrial setting.

 Don't leave without picking up a loaf of own-made sourdough

Rather than serving just one house coffee, the team provide two main options: a bespoke blend from Manchester's Heart and Graft and a rotating single-origin espresso from Square Mile in London. Adventurous sippers can expand their horizons further via European guest roasts from the likes of Gardelli, The Barn and Manhattan.

The international theme continues in a Mediterranean-inspired brunch menu where everything – from pesto, sauces and tapenade to sourdough, cakes and pastries – is made in-house.

Established
2022

Key roastery
Multiple roasteries

Brewing method
Espresso, batch brew, Clever Dripper

Machine
La Marzocco Linea PB

Grinder
Victoria Arduino Mythos One

Opening hours
Mon-Fri
8am-4pm
Sat
9am-4pm
Sun
10am-4pm

Salford

35 Bold Street Coffee – Spinningfields

2 Hardman Street, Manchester, M3 3HF

boldstreetcoffee.co.uk

 bold.streetcoffee boldstreetcoffee

This latest addition to the BSC family specialises in satiating caffeine geeks and hungry commuters with its brews, Grab & Go menu and in-house bakes.

While the fresh (yet fast) food is great, this is still very much a coffee-focused site. To prove it, the team have installed a swish Tone Touch 03, a new automated pourover machine that's one of only a few in the whole of the North.

☕ For a next-level brew experience, ask for your coffee brewed via Tone Swiss

Roasting their own beans in the heart of Liverpool, the Bold Street roasting team supply the five cafes across Liverpool and Manchester with deliciously fresh beans. However, they also like to spread the love by showcasing other roasting talents, including Origo, The Barn, Sumo, Newground, Dark Arts, North Star, Red Bank, Assembly and Fort.

The Bold Street crew have increased their own-brand coffee selection (with all coffees available to order online) to align with their new coffee subscription service for espresso, filter and decaf. Branded merch is also sold on the site – the Just Brew It tee is epic.

Established
2024

Key roastery
Bold Street Coffee

Brewing method
Espresso, pourover, batch filter

Machine
La Marzocco Linea PB

Grinder
Compak E8

Opening hours
Mon-Fri
7am-6pm

Manchester

Federal – Deansgate

194 Deansgate, Manchester, M3 3ND
federalcafe.co.uk | 01618 330890
 federalcafebar federalcafebar

Whether you're itching for a barista-quality flat white or fancy a bite to eat somewhere cheerful, we'd recommend taking a trip to sunny Melbourne for an hour via this Manchester institution.

Inspired by the brunch and brew scene down under, the dishes at Federal are always vibrant, the coffee expertly extracted and the rosettas impeccably poured. Every caffeinated sip on the extensive menu is concocted from single-origin beans roasted by Ozone, including seasonal specials such as the black-sesame latte, iced dirty chai and hot Milo. Regulars can't get enough of the coffee and some are known to return three times a day for a Federal fix.

The denim aprons worn by the team are made by owner Claudio's 90-year-old gran

Deansgate is perma-busy, so expect queues (the cafe doesn't do reservations), but don't be deterred as they move quickly and the team have been known to hand out hot chocolate – and umbrellas when needed – to those waiting.

Once it's your turn, hit up the likes of the house-fave french toast, or steak and eggs served with Fed sauce and salsa verde – paired, of course, with an expertly prepared brew.

Established
2019

Key roastery
Ozone Coffee

Brewing method
Espresso, filter, batch brew

Machine
La Marzocco Linea PB

Grinder
Mahlkonig E80

Opening hours
Mon-Fri
7.30am-4pm
Sat-Sun
8am-5pm

Manchester

(37) Atrium Coffee

1 St Peter's Square, Manchester, M2 3DE

atrium-coffee.co.uk

atriumcoffeemcr

After climbing the coffee ladder for ten years – moving from barista to wholesale manager – it was only a matter of time before Nat McDonald took the leap and made real his dream of opening his own coffee shop. In 2022 he launched Atrium in central Manchester.

The light-filled space has become a hub for a coffee-loving community who visit to hang out and indulge their passion for seriously good speciality. It's no surprise the pours are so pro as, in 2022, Nat won the Barista League UK competition. His first-place prize was a trip to Colombia where he visited different coffee farms and experienced life at origin. Customers hunt out Atrium to experience his 'spro skills for themselves.

Nat is one of the brains behind the coffee trail, Slurp Fest

A sublime house espresso is provided by Swan Song, while guest roasts are sourced from the likes of Harmony, A.M.O.C and Oddy Knocky. Nat has a close relationship with Colombian coffee producers Johnny Martinez of El Jaragual and Wilton Benitez of Granja Paraiso 92, and tries wherever possible to showcase their coffees on his brew bar. While the espresso drinks are flawless, the hypnotic pourovers are a must-try house speciality, revealing the coffees' various and nuanced flavours.

Regular coffee-focused events, tailored to all members of the coffee community, are held at Atrium – stay up-to-date with what's coming up on socials.

Established
2022

Key roastery
Swan Song
Coffee Roasters

Brewing method
Espresso, Orea, V60

Machine
Victoria Arduino
Eagle One

Grinder
Mahlkonig E65S GbW,
Mahlkonig EK43,
Victoria Arduino
Mythos One

Opening hours
Mon
8am-2.30pm
Tue-Thu
8am-4pm
Fri
8am-2.30pm

Manchester

70

Just Natas

Unit fc2 Arndale Market, 49 High Street, Manchester, M4 3AH

justnatas.com | 07539 581801

justnatas just_natas

It's a bold move to focus on just two items – there's nowhere to hide if they're anything less than exceptional – but the team at Just Natas pull it off with aplomb.

Squeezed between the street-food stalls at Arndale Market, this tiny venue serves one of southern Europe's most iconic food and drink pairings: pastel de nata and syrupy espresso. The traditional Portuguese custard tarts are baked fresh each morning, giving early birds the opportunity to snaffle them still warm from the oven, crunching through flaky pastry to an oozing centre.

🛈 Look out for limited-edition pastel de natas every weekend

A crema-rich espresso is the pastry's traditional accompaniment and the Just Natas baristas deliver perfect shots using beans from London roastery Ozone. Add steamed milk for a sweeter serve or even a dose of chocolate for a moreish mocha.

On weekends, the bakers get creative with the custard tarts and craft special-edition fillings such as Biscoff, espresso chocolate, and blueberry and white chocolate. The Manchester Tart is a returning special which features ripples of raspberry jam in the middle and a crown of toasted coconut and cherry.

Established
2020

Key roastery
Ozone Coffee

Brewing method
Espresso

Machine
La Marzocco GS3

Grinder
Mythos One

Opening hours
Mon-Sat
10am-5pm
Sun
11.30am-4pm

Manchester

(39) Federal – Northern Quarter

9 Nicholas Croft, Northern Quarter, Manchester, M4 1EY
federalcafe.co.uk | 01614 250974

 federalcafebar federalcafebar

This supernova of the Manchester speciality scene has been the place for on-point espresso and sweet-as french toast for over a decade.

The popularity of its Aussie-inspired coffee offering and all-day brunch menus have resulted in four Federal outposts in Manchester, as well as sister brands Just Natas (the go-to for silky espresso and golden-topped pastel de nata in Arndale Market) and the Federal Coffee Cart in Altrincham.

Need a new reusable? Get the Federal KeepCup and score 10 per cent off your takeaway coffees

This Northern Quarter spot is perma-busy, so arrive early to secure a table. Order a flat white made with beans from London's Ozone to sip while you peruse a bill of foodie thrills. The flagship dish is french toast piled with the likes of macerated berries, white chocolate, almond crumble, whipped vanilla mascarpone and salted caramel, but you won't be disappointed if you take a savoury route and plump for halloumi and mushrooms with poachies and dukkah on sourdough, or turkish eggs with hot chilli butter and za'atar.

Marry your menu selection with a fruity batch brew or take a detour via the cocktail list and toast your brunch with a Bloody Mary or Espresso Martini.

Established
2014

Key roastery
Ozone Coffee

Brewing method
Espresso,
filter, batch brew

Machine
La Marzocco Linea PB

Grinder
Mahlkonig E80

Opening hours
Mon-Fri
7.30am-4pm
Sat-Sun
8am-5pm

Manchester

72

Hampton & Voúis

78-88 High Street, Manchester, M4 1ES

hamptonandvouis.co.uk

hamptonandvouis hamptonandvouis

The Northern Quarter crowd have bagged themselves a new brunch hangout in this sister site to the OG on Princess Street. Regulars will already be familiar with its first-rate coffee and excellent food, which is made from scratch each day using only the freshest ingredients.

The plant-based french toast is particularly loved and comes in three guises: Biscoff; caramel apple and cinnamon; and peanut butter and banana. Squishy vegan pancakes loaded with indulgent toppings and refreshing smoothie bowls also feature.

Those who sway towards the savoury side will also find satiation on the all-day brunch menu: delicious picks include toasted sourdough piled with serrano ham, red pesto, mozzarella and poached eggs.

Accompanying these brunch plates is a nutty Buxton-roasted espresso, and fruity single-origin guest beans worked into whistle-clean batch brews.

If you try one thing, make it the vegan french toast

If you see a jar of Greek thyme honey for sale on the counter, get in there quickly and buy it. The nectarous liquid gold comes from the Voúis family's land on the Greek island of Kalymnos and is favoured for its flavour and potential immunity-strengthening powers. The jars are replenished each summer, but when they're gone they're gone for another year.

Established
2024

Key roastery
Buxton Coffee Roasters

Brewing method
Espresso, batch brew

Machine
Sanremo D8

Grinder
Mahlkonig E65S GbW

Opening hours
Mon-Sun
9am-4pm

Manchester

SEESAW

86 Princess Street, Manchester, M1 6NG

seesawspace.com | 01618 060871

 seesawspace seesawspacecafe

Surrounded by university buildings, start-ups and global businesses, Seesaw's historical warehouse – which incorporates a workspace, cafe and events area – is at the epicentre of Manchester's creative scene. It also has one of the best views in the city.

Tastemakers are drawn to the hub to catch exhibitions from up-and-coming artists, practise sun salutations in yoga classes, take part in coffee cuppings, and to link up with likeminded folk at social events. Most importantly, however, they swing by to sip exceptionally crafted single-origin coffee in cool surrounds.

Thumb through new-release hardbacks in the bookshop and pick out prints in the art store

As might be expected in a cafe that celebrates innovation, the carefully considered coffee is the result of collaborative partnerships with indie roasteries. Beans from Red Bank plus a rotation of guest roasts (think Hard Lines, We Are Here and Coffee Collective) are crafted into espresso and filter brews that shine in clarity.

Visitors don't have to work in the creative industries to relish a brew in a space that blurs the line between work and play. However, they shouldn't be surprised if the inspiring atmosphere and quality caffeine put a revitalised spring in their step.

Established
2021

Key roastery
Red Bank
Coffee Roasters

Brewing method
Espresso, batch brew,
Clever Dripper,
cold brew, V60

Machine
La Marzocco Strada

Grinder
Mahlkonig E65S GbW,
Mahlkonig EK43 S,
Victoria Arduino
Mythos One

Opening hours
Mon-Fri
8.30am-4pm

Manchester

Federal – Oxford Road

Unit B2-2, Circle Square, Oxford Road, Manchester, M1 7FS

federalcafe.co.uk | 01614 250974

 federalcafebar federalcafebar

The newest Federal outpost opened on Oxford Road in 2022 and attracts a constant stream of discerning coffee drinkers who visit to top up their caffeine quota and feast on contemporary brunch plates.

It's the busiest cafe in the Federal family, always filled with locals grabbing coffee on their way to work, students nourishing body and soul with vibrant eats between seminars, and tourists who've made the trip to soak up the neighbourhood vibes and dig into the legendary french toast.

The quality single-origin coffee fuelling the buzzy chatter is roasted by Ozone. Whether your order is a short black or an iced mocha with a shot of syrup, you'll find it crafted with care and cheery service by the skilled baristas.

⚡ Switch up your usual espresso order and plump for a juicy batch brew

Power up for the day ahead with the likes of pan-fried halloumi, garlic and thyme-roasted mushrooms, poached eggs, Fed sauce and dukkah, all piled on sourdough. No plans for the rest of the day? Match your brunch pick with a Bloody Mary.

Those looking for a quick bite and coffee hit should take advantage of the bagel and brew offer (available until midday) and get an egg, avo or bacon bagel and a hot drink to-go.

Established
2022

Key roastery
Ozone Coffee

Brewing method
Espresso, filter, batch brew

Machine
La Marzocco Linea PB

Grinder
Mahlkonig E80

Opening hours
Mon-Fri
7.30am-4pm
Sat-Sun
8am-5pm

Manchester

43 The Frostery Living

11 King Street, Delph, Oldham, Greater Manchester, OL3 5DL

frosteryliving.co.uk | 01457 879883

f frosteryliving ◎ frosteryliving

'Why should the cool shops always be in the urban districts of town?' is the question The Frostery Living founders Suzanne and James Thorp found themselves asking. Not coming up with a good enough answer, in 2022 they decided to defy convention and launch their lifestyle store, coffee shop and cakery in the village of Delph.

The pair had a vision of bringing a different kind of lifestyle shopping experience to the area: one that also folded exquisite coffee and carbs into the mix. The result is a curated space that celebrates all things artisan, handmade and beautifully crafted.

ⓘ A creative workshop space on the first floor is available to hire

Visit to browse lust-worthy homewares and books before hitting the espresso bar for a North Star coffee and the tough job of deciding which masterfully baked cake to pair with it.

Anyone would struggle to contain their greed when faced with baked goods of this calibre. Suzanne's experience in the upper echelons of cakemaking has been documented on Channel 4's *Extreme Cake Makers*. She's been a judge at cake competitions worldwide, won a plethora of awards and also runs separate celebration-cake business The Frostery. Everything on the cake counter – from the almond slices to the fruity Delph ladybirds – is freshly made at her bakery in neighbouring Uppermill and served exclusively at this hybrid cafe.

Established
2022

Key roastery
North Star
Coffee Roasters

Brewing method
Expresso, filter

Machine
La Marzocco
Linea Classic S

Grinder
Anfim Pratica

Opening hours
Wed-Sat
10am-4pm
Sun
11am-3pm

Oldham

44 Weaver & Wilde

42 High Street, Uppermill, Saddleworth, Greater Manchester, OL3 6HA

weaverandwilde.co.uk | 01457 878725

 weaverandwilde weaver_and_wilde

In the centre of the village of Uppermill, Weaver & Wilde's MO is brunch-scoffing by day and speciality-steak feasting by night.

The award-winning business upped sticks and moved to larger premises at the end of 2023, which has given them more space for their coffee house and steak-restaurant concept. Despite the high quality of the brews and seasonal British food, this is an unpretentious spot: the aim is simply to have guests leave with their caffeine quota maxed and their hunger satiated.

For the signature W&W experience try the 1kg 60-day, dry-aged tomahawk steak

The coffee is carefully crafted from beans roasted down the road at Dark Woods (ethically sourced in direct partnership with farmers at source) while milk is supplied by McLinktock's Dairy, whose herd grazes on Saddleworth grass in Denshaw. A miscellany of guest roasteries are woven in on a rotational basis, with seasonal single origins used for filter and drip serves. Visiting with a tea drinker? They'll appreciate the high-quality selection crafted by Tea Keepers in Stalybridge.

Weaver & Wilde recently launched a sister site, Blackbird & Wilde, just down the road. The coffee house and pizzeria deals in slurps and artisan slices.

Established
2019

Key roastery
Dark Woods Coffee

Brewing method
Espresso, filter, V60

Machine
La Marzocco Linea PB

Grinder
Anfim Pratica

Opening hours
Mon-Wed
8am-5pm
Thu-Sat
8am-11pm
Sun
8am-6pm

Saddleworth

CAKESMITHS
FOR COFFEE SHOPS

GREAT
COFFEE SHOPS
DESERVE
GREAT
CAKE.

TRY US FOR FREE AT
CAKESMITHS.COM

AWARD-WINNING | MADE BY HAND | NEXT DAY DELIVERY

Dandelion

5 Grove Parade, Buxton, Derbyshire, SK17 6AJ

dandelionbuxton

BEEN THERE • BEEN THERE • BEEN THERE • BEEN THERE •

The attention poured into a coffee experience can turn it from 'good' to 'great', and that's certainly the case at Dandelion. The Buxton coffee shop prides itself on giving its customers a bespoke and beautifully crafted caffeinated experience every time.

The care the team take in sourcing and brewing speciality coffee is as clear to see in their curated coffee menu as it is in the impeccable espresso and filter serves.

🕊 Keep 'em peeled for a Dandelion farm shop offering high-welfare dairy and products from local artisans

Rather than sticking to a single house roastery, Dandelion serves a wide selection of beans from a smorgasbord of international roasteries. The cafe also carries an exciting range of frozen rare beans that span diverse origins, processes and price points. Coffee is sourced based on its quality and whether it brings something new and notable to the tasting table, so don't be surprised to find Cup of Excellence winners rubbing shoulders with dark-horse gems from lesser-known roasteries and origins.

This obsessive approach also manifests itself in the brewing process, which is uncompromising: the baristas take time to ensure every pour is top-notch, so it's worth allowing yourself time to slow down and savour each sip. Happily, while the standards are high, the vibe is tranquil instead of preachy.

Established
2023

Key roastery
Multiple roasteries

Brewing method
Espresso, pourover, batch filter, cold brew

Machine
La Marzocco Linea Classic

Grinder
Compak PK100

Opening hours
Mon-Tue
8am-4pm
Fri-Sat
8am-6pm

Buxton

AREA 1

ROAST
-ERIES

Rinaldo's Speciality Coffee & Fine Teas

Unit 12 Lakeland Food Park, Crook Road, Kendal, Cumbria, LA8 8QJ

rinscoffee.com | 01539 592587

 rinscoffee rinscoffee

© Stuart Thomson

This Kendal roastery and espresso bar is worth seeking out for its dedication to small-batch sourcing of sustainably farmed and flavoursome coffees. Visiting locals and online customers face the difficult decision of choosing between Great Taste award-winning house blend Casa (a mix of Brazilian and El Salvadoran beans) and the newer and fruitier house blend Chameleon.

'Time and effort have been spent carefully cupping, sourcing and roasting beans to do the farmers' hard work justice'

There's also a weekly rotation of single-origin beans from South America, Africa and Asia to agonise over, including a Great Taste award-winning Burundi from a women's co-operative in Bujumbura. Whatever the final pick, sippers can be assured that much time and effort has been spent carefully sourcing, roasting and cupping the beans to do the farmers' hard work justice.

As well as crafting a great offering of coffees on their Giesen W15A, the team source and sell an assortment of loose-leaf teas. Both coffee and teas can be ordered for next-day delivery via the website or sampled at the roastery's espresso bar and shop — which also offers the opportunity to drool over a display of Sanremo and ECM machines.

Established
2015

Roaster make & size
Giesen W15A 15kg

Kendal

Podda & Wren Coffee Roasters

4 Elephant Yard, Kendal, Cumbria, LA9 4QQ

podda-wren.co.uk | 01539 272144

 poddaandwren

SIPPED THAT · SIPPED THAT · SIPPED THAT · SIPPED THAT

© Jumpy James

Kendal's Podda & Wren made a dynamic debut in 2022, driven by a deep passion for plant-based living, a commitment to sustainability and the spirit of innovation.

The team's operations are powered by a cutting-edge, fully electric Typhoon Fluid Bed roaster, bringing a modern touch to their craft. The contact-free air roasting technology ensures consistency and a clean, bright taste in every bean, highlighting the unique flavours developed at source and honouring the hard work of farmers.

'Plant-based passion, a sustainable spirit and innovative energy'

The core range of coffees (primarily single origin) is sourced from Brazil, Uganda and Colombia, complemented by a rotating selection of micro-lots from around the globe. These limited-edition coffees, from places like East Timor, Myanmar, Ethiopia, Thailand, Costa Rica and Guatemala, are refreshed every six to eight weeks.

The team's first foray into blending resulted in Fellside, a light roast with notes of chocolate and syrup. It's inspired by the coffee that co-founder Jonathan Wren served from his first coffee van, a fixture still supplying exceptional brews and plant-based cakes at events across the Lake District.

For a taste of the expertly crafted coffees, visit the on-site espresso bar where drinks are served with Moma Barista Oat milk as standard, in keeping with Podda & Wren's plant-based ethos.

Established
2022

Roaster make & size
Typhoon Shoproaster 5kg

Kendal

48 Red Bank Coffee Roasters

Red Bank's rep for cooking up sustainably and ethically sourced beans in Kendal just got a green glow-up thanks to its installation of a new eco-friendly Loring S35 Kestral roaster. Bag beans and merch via the website.

Unit 12 Boundary Bank, Kendal, Cumbria, LA9 5RR

redbankcoffee.com 🅞 redbankcoffee

Atkinsons Coffee Roasters

12 China Street, Lancaster, Lancashire, LA1 1EX

thecoffeehopper.com | 01524 65470

atkinsonscoffee atkinsons.coffee

Tradition meets innovation at this historic coffee roastery in the heart of Lancaster. Originally established in 1837 as The Grasshopper Tea House, Atkinsons is one of the oldest roasteries in the UK.

Since taking over in 2005, Ian and Sue Steel (pictured) have reinvigorated the brand and dragged it into the 21st century. Today it's one of the most respected speciality roasters in the country, renowned for its reliably delicious blends and revolving seasonal single origins which are roasted on a super-low-emission Loring Kestrel.

'One of the most respected speciality roasters in the country'

For almost two decades, the Atkinsons team have been dedicated to building long-lasting relationships with producers around the world, including in Guatemala, Brazil, Ethiopia, Costa Rica, Sumatra, Rwanda and Colombia. A particularly close partnership with Café Granja La Esperanza in Colombia results in a regular delivery of rare and interesting varietals which have been processed using different fermentation methods.

The best place to sample Atkinsons beans is at one of its three excellent cafes in Lancaster. Pay a visit to The Hall on China Street to taste the brews and own-baked carbs before browsing coffees and artisan goods in the original shop next door. Coffee-curious folk and wholesale customers can explore behind the scenes at the roastery's new training room.

Established
1837

Roaster make & size
Loring S35 Kestrel
35kg

Lancaster

Neighbourhood Coffee

Unit 22 Sandon Estate, Sandon Way, Liverpool, Merseyside, L5 9YN

neighbourhoodcoffee.co.uk | 01512 366741

◼ neighbourhoodcoffee ◎ neighbourhoodcoffee

Nothing lifts the spirits like belting out an 80s classic, and this Liverpool roastery's beans — which take their names from smash hits of that era — provide the perfect prompt for those in need of a perk-me-up while preparing their morning brew.

Headlining the collection is West Blend Girls (a house blend that's also available in Nespresso-compatible pods), with support from the likes of Born Sippin' (a light natural Ethiopian) and Kiss From A Roast (a rich washed Indian). Even the decaf, The Way You Mocha Me Feel, delivers a dose of musical nostalgia.

'There isn't much about the farm-to-cup experience they don't know'

While founders and former green-bean buyers Edward and Chris like to keep things creative, their core focus is on crafting high-quality, accessible coffee. Their shared knowledge, combined with that of their diverse team, means there isn't much about the farm-to-cup experience they don't know and they're happy to share this expertise with customers.

The team have scooped multiple Great Taste awards over the past three years, and their range includes at least eight award-winning roasts. Subscriptions cater for those looking for convenience and includes a Roaster's Choice option which showcases exclusive one-off coffees. Want to get lost down the coffee rabbit hole? Book onto a barista training course or an in-depth brewing class.

Established
2014

Roaster make & size
Giesen W60A 60kg,
Giesen W15A 15kg

Liverpool

51 Crosby Coffee Roasters

13 Glegg Street, Liverpool, Merseyside, L3 7DX
crosbycoffee.co.uk | 01515 385454

crosbycoffee crosbycoffeeltd

After celebrating their tenth birthday last year, it's all change at Crosby Coffee. The team relocated from their original HQ to new premises a couple of years ago, but have since set up in another new spot – this time inside a former cotton mill on Glegg Street. Three roasters are situated across three floors, plus the significant space also holds a training area. It's in this dedicated training room that pros and the public can perfect the crafts of manual brewing, latte art, sensory skills and milk texturing.

'Keep 'em peeled for the on-site coffee shop that's opening soon'

The capacious new location has enabled the team to install a hefty state-of-the-art Loring S35 Kestrel. The machine bronzes an ever-growing range of blends and single-origin beans that hail from far-flung corners of the world including Brazil, Ethiopia, Colombia, Honduras, Mexico, Kenya, Uganda and Guatemala.

Beans are sustainably and directly sourced from farmers, and the signature Iron Men blend fuses beans from Guatemala, Honduras and Brazil into a rich and smooth concoction with notes of hazelnut and dark chocolate.

The Crosby crew don't like to rest on their laurels and recently helped set up a charity football tournament in the area, their own team comprised of Crosby staff and those from their wholesale partners. They're also in the process of opening a coffee shop within the roastery.

Established
2014

Roaster make & size
Loring S35
Kestral 35kg,
Toper 30 30kg,
Toper 10 10kg

Liverpool

Two Brothers — Roastery

Warrington Market, 2 Times Square, Warrington, Cheshire, WA1 2NT

twobrothers.coffee

f twobrotherscoffeeltd twobrotherscoffee

Brothers, best buds and self-proclaimed coffee geeks Steve and Dave are electrical engineers by trade but turned their passion for speciality coffee into a business when they launched Two Brothers in 2017.

In 2020 they expanded the roastery operation and moved into this Warrington site, where they've developed a coffee-loving community who frequent the HQ roastery-cafe to watch beans being roasted while they sip. Visit the Two Brothers coffee shops in Altrincham and Ormskirk for more caffeinated thrills.

The bros believe coffee is best shared with friends — which includes the coffee farmers with whom they enjoy good relationships and the cafe's band of customers.

'Greens are stored inside a lovingly restored antique ticket booth'

Beans are sourced from across the globe. When they arrive, the greens are stored inside a lovingly restored antique ticket booth (rescued from a skip when the Warrington Baths was demolished) before being roasted to produce the likes of Transient. This all-rounder house roast yields notes of hazelnut, milk choc and cola, and is used in espresso drinks across the Two Brothers collective. The blend changes seasonally to include lots from the likes of The Cocatrel Cooperative in Brazil.

Established
2017

Roaster make & size
Giesen W15 15kg
Aillio Bullet 1kg

Oddy Knocky Coffee

Unit 16 Spring Street Business Park, St Marks Street, Bolton,

Greater Manchester, BL3 6NR | oddyknockycoffee.co.uk | 01204 783078

oddyknockycoffee oddyknockycoffee

Oddy Knocky exploded onto the coffee scene in 2023 and has become a favourite among speciality fans for its promotion of zero pretension and sod-all snobbery. The roastery's tagline: 'brewing in the face of boring', says it all – the team are interested only in creating damn fine coffee for all, no matter the sippers' coffee knowledge or experience.

Refusing to allow the speciality coffee industry to close its doors to anyone, Oddy Knocky has built a community centred around the drink they love so much. An elitist coffee club, this ain't.

'The roastery's tagline "brewing in the face of boring" says it all'

With a something-for-everyone attitude, the Oddy Knocky range includes a crowd-pleasing house blend which the team describe as *'a solid coffee shop classic'*, alongside bestseller Caramel Kush (a natural Ethiopian with tasting notes of caramel, green apple and candied almonds) and an ever-rotating line-up of single origins.

There's also an exciting ever-changing range of filter coffees which, to date, has included coffee from renowned producers Nestor Lasso, Sebastian Ramirez and the Arcila family.

Established
2023

Roaster make & size
Giesen 15kg

Bolton

54 Bohee Coffee

Unit C1 Kestrel Court, Kestrel Road, Trafford Park, Manchester, M17 1SF

bohee.coffee | 01618 189919

boheecoffee

This ethical roastery only deals in beans that are sustainably sourced and of superlative quality. Founder and chief roaster Chris brought his sourcing know-how and finely tuned palate from speciality tea business Bohea Teas to coffee, scouring countries including Kenya and Colombia for morally sound lots with exciting qualities.

Chris procures beans in tune with the season and harvest, however, his range always includes two regional coffees from Brazil and Guatemala. Not only does this give customers the guarantee of delicious drops from those two countries, but also provides the farmers with an assured income.

'A quality and ethics-led attitude to sourcing'

Constantly changing single origins on the seasonal line-up have included a washed and extended-fermentation coffee from Mexico, a process which highlights intriguing flavours. Visit the Bohee Cafe in Chorlton to sample the latest beans via a wide selection of brew methods (including two espresso options, a rotating batch brew, and a wildcard pourover) and to feast on contemporary brunch plates.

With such a quality and ethics-led attitude to sourcing, it's no surprise these guys strive to minimise their environmental impact wherever possible. Recyclable packaging is used for beans sold on-site and online, while the team also contribute positively to their own community and the regions from which they source.

Courses and roastery tours are available by appointment.

Established
2022

Roaster make & size
Giesen W15A 15kg

Manchester

55 **Django Coffee Co.**

Unit 5, 58-60 Higher Ardwick, Manchester, M12 6DA
djangocoffeeco.com | 01617 061457

 djangocoffeeco djangocoffeeco

The beating heart of this roastery is its focus on forging transparent and fair direct-trade relationships with farmers across the world. The roasting crew are uber conscientious about buying only the very best speciality beans, so every lot is ethically sourced and 100 per cent traceable.

'The roasting style never ventures beyond a medium profile'

'We believe sustainability is hugely important in the production of quality coffee,' says owner Ste Paweleck. 'We want to minimise our carbon footprint and ensure each stage of the coffee chain – from harvesting to roasting – is carried out with the kind of knowledge and understanding that does justice to everyone involved.'

The roasting style never ventures beyond a medium profile, due to the team's belief that single-origin coffees benefit from lighter roast profiles. Recently, they launched their first espresso blends. Moderat (crafted from two Ugandan coffees) is a full-bodied all-rounder while Extrawelt (combining natural Ugandan maliba and washed Rwandan gitwe beans) packs a velvety punch. As you'd expect from this environmentally conscious roastery, beans are processed in the most sustainable way possible.

Established
2015

Roaster make & size
Giesen W15A 15kg

Manchester

56 Kickback Coffee

Unit 3 The Old Brickworks, Bakestonedale Road, Pott Shrigley,
Cheshire, SK10 5RX | kickbackcoffee.co.uk | 01625 409616

kickbackcoffee

© Rob Montandon

Every cup of Kickback Coffee is imbued with a spirit of adventure, inspired by the great outdoors and driven by a passion for exceptional brews.

In the eight years since founder Alex Shaw launched the indie roastery in the heart of the Peak District, a faithful community of outdoor enthusiasts – united by their love of speciality coffee and nature – has formed and continues to flourish.

At Kickback's espresso bar and roastery space in The Old Brickworks in Cheshire, intrepid explorers and caffeine-loving locals drop in to sample the latest beans which have finished resting after a spell in one of the high-spec Giesen roasters.

'Every cup of Kickback Coffee is imbued with a spirit of adventure'

The roastery's signature blend, The Explorer, creates a bold-yet-balanced brew that's lusciously smooth with a nutty flavour and hint of raisin sweetness. Whether knocked back to fuel the next hike or sipped as a post-ride pick-me-up, it's a stonking brew for adventurers.

The team are dedicated to looking after the planet and minimising their environmental impact. To help reduce the roastery's carbon footprint, local coffee deliveries are made using an Urban Arrow e-cargo bike.

Established
2017

Roaster make & size
Giesen W15 15kg,
Giesen W30 30kg

Pott Shrigley

93

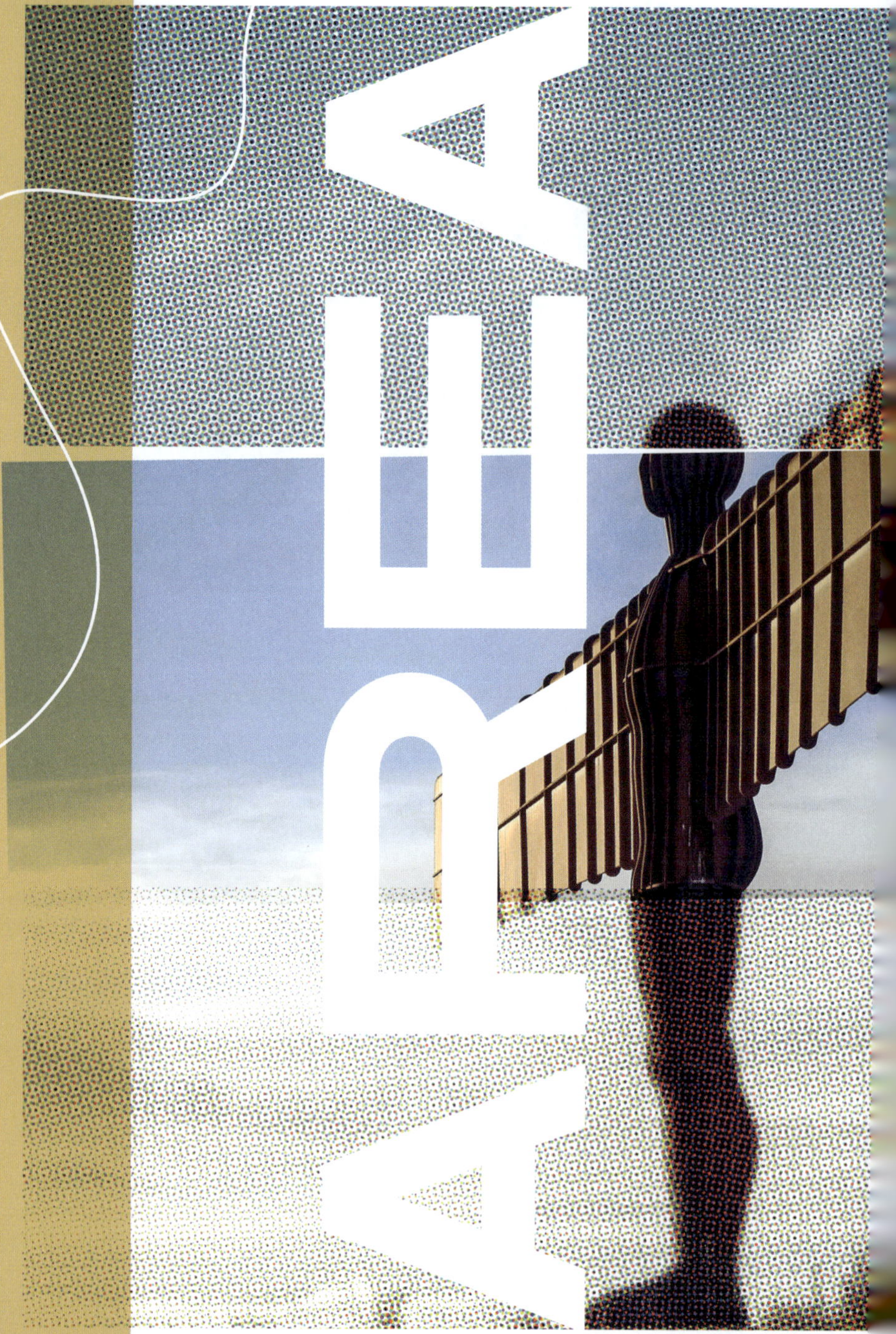
AREA

2

Area 2

● Coffee shops

1 PureKnead Bakery
2 Rustic Cup
3 Lagom Speciality Coffee Bar
4 Sorcerer
5 Harvest
6 Local NCL
7 Pink Lane Cafe
8 Flat White Kitchen
9 The Seahorse Coffee Box
10 Mr Cooper's Coffee House – Bedford Street
11 Scoundrels Coffee Co.
12 Mr Cooper's Coffee House – Church Street
13 Koda
14 Roost Coffee – Espresso Bar
15 Kinship
16 Rise – York
17 Heppni Bakeri
18 Still

● Roasteries

50 Pink Lane Coffee
51 Ouseburn Coffee Co.
52 Rounton Coffee Roasters
53 Roost Coffee & Roastery

Locations are approximate

Northumberland
National Park

7

6

5

2

4 51   Whitley Bay

3 50   1

NEWCASTLE

SUNDERLAND

8

DURHAM

North
Pennines
National
Landscape

Seaton Carew

9

Middlesbrough

10

11

Saltburn-by-the-sea   Whitby

52   12

Northallerton

North York Moors
National Park

Scarborough

13

Howardian Hills
National Landscape   53   Malton

14

Nidderdale
National
Landscape

Driffield

17

YORK   15

16

Find cafes and
roasteries in this
area on page 98

HULL

18

Area 2

● Coffee shops

● Roasteries

● Coffee trainer

Locations are approximate

Nidderdale
National
Landscape

54

21

20

Skipton

Addingham

Knaresborough

19

Harrogate

Haworth

Shipley

LEEDS
(See city map on p101)

BRADFORD

Hebden Bridge

32

Halifax

57

Cleckheaton

56

33

36

63

Lindley

35

45

34

Huddersfield

Lingards Wood

58

Honley

38

37

59

39

Marsden

Holmfirth

60

Barnsley

40

Penistone

41

Stocksbridge

42

47

46

62

44

61

SHEFFIELD

43

48

49

Peak District
National Park

MENU

ESPRESSO	3
PICCOLO	3.5
CAPPUCCINO	4
LATTE	4.5
MOCHA	5
AMERICANO	3.5
FILTER	3.25
TEA	3

LEEDS

● Coffee shops

22 Rabbit Hole Coffee
23 Fika North
24 Bowery
25 Coffee On The Crescent
26 Stage Espresso & Brew Bar
27 Kapow Coffee
28 Laynes
29 Archive
30 Galleria
31 The Hideout @ Harper Farm

● Roasteries

55 North Star Coffee Roasters

Locations are approximate

Moortown

22

Far Headingly

23

24

Headingly

Hawksworth

Kirkstall

Chapeltown

25

Hyde Park

Little London

29

26 LEEDS

27

30

28

55

Armley

Holbeck

Whitehall Ind Estate

31

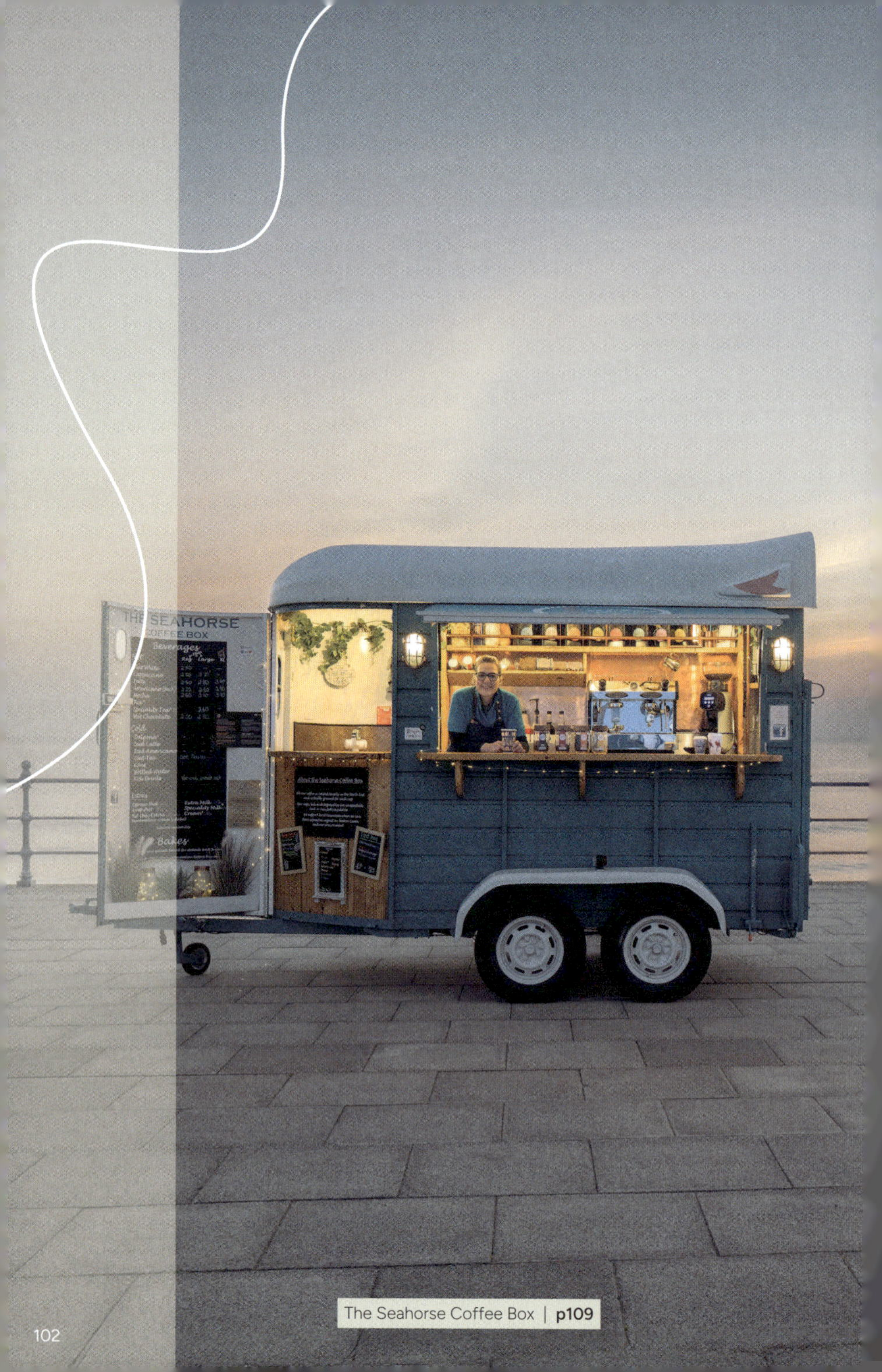

The Seahorse Coffee Box | **p109**

AREA 2
COFFEE SHOPS

PureKnead Bakery

(1)

111-113 Park View, Whitley Bay, Tyne and Wear, NE26 3RH

pure-knead.co.uk | 07964 864181

Purekneadbakery

Baking may be fundamentally scientific, but cast your eye over the cakes and pastries adorning the PureKnead counter and you may conclude their creator must surely be an artist ... and you'd be right.

In 2015, returning to work after the birth of her children, fine-art graduate Paula Watson committed to putting her creative degree to gastronomic use. She started with a cake stall at Tynemouth Market and, after 18 months of successful trading, moved her flourishing business to a vacant shop in Whitley Bay.

⚡ Word on the street is that PureKnead's third coffee shop will open later this year

More than eight years on, PureKnead is famous in the seaside town – and beyond – for its viennoiserie, 48-hour sourdough and bespoke custom bakes and while the ingredients are local, much of the inspiration is international. Regulars queue down the street for Copenhagen-inspired pastries and antipodean classics.

Coffee drinkers can be assured the brews are as good as the bakes: a bank of excellent baristas deliver consistently silky pours using the house coffee which is roasted by Assembly.

Established
2016

Key roastery
Assembly Coffee

Brewing method
Espresso, pourover

Machine
Victoria Arduino

Grinder
Mythos

Opening hours
Mon-Sun
9am-3pm

Whitley Bay

(2) Rustic Cup

28 Park View, Whitley Bay, Tyne and Wear, NE26 2TH

rusticcup.co.uk

f rusticcup.uk rusticcup.uk

Whether you're nipping in to grab beans to brew at home or settling in for brunch, you're assured a warm welcome and fantastic coffee at Rustic Cup.

Before moving to the North East and establishing their own venue, Lee Coates and Veronika Pitakova (the globetrotting bikers behind this cafe) explored coffee culture at its source, which included growing beans in Timor-Leste and mastering brewing techniques in Italy. The result is a coffee offering bursting with passion and expertise.

Hit up one of the free cupping sessions and expand your coffee-drinking horizons

The crew utilise a range of brewing methods including espresso, AeroPress and Chemex to deliver meticulously prepped coffees crafted from Baristocracy beans. While espresso is the most popular method on the menu, the barista team include an award-winning filter-brewing pro so factor that in when choosing your serve style.

Rustic Cup's foodie offering is designed to lift the spirits and includes ciabatta rolls crammed with Whitley Bay produce, plus smoothie bowls and salads in a kaleidoscope of colours and fresh flavours. Add craft beers, wines and an impressive cocktail list to the mix and it's easy to see how an early brunch at Rustic Cup could easily turn into a rather long lunch.

Established
2020

Key roastery
Baristocracy Coffee Roasters

Brewing method
Espresso, AeroPress, batch filter, Chemex, V60

Machine
La Marzocco KB90 ABR

Grinder
Mahlkonig E65S GbW x2, Mahlkonig EK43 S, Mythos One

Opening hours
Mon-Sat
7.30am-5pm
Sun
9am-4pm

Whitley Bay

Lagom Speciality Coffee Bar

8 Monk Street, Newcastle, Tyne and Wear, NE5 4EP

◎ lagomcoffeebar

The Swedish term *lagom* is used to describe an amount or state that's just right: not too little or too much of anything, but in the balanced sweet spot that elicits contentment. It's a principle that's woven through every element of Newcastle's Scandi-inspired coffee bar.

Nothing embodies *lagom* quite like this cafe's coffee offering. Thanks to its wide range of carefully procured beans and team of dexterous baristas pulling the shots, this is a place to slow down and savour every drop. Knocking back one too many 'spros till the shakes kick in definitely isn't the vibe.

⚡ Ask for a split shot – cortado served alongside an espresso – to sample the beans in black and white

Pourover coffees are the star of the show and served with pin-sharp precision. Two filter options are changed monthly to keep the offering fresh and highlight new flavoursome finds from across the coffee-growing belt. There are also always two single-origin coffees to sample as espresso, the beans sourced from Fika and other celebrated roasteries in the UK and beyond. To delve deeper into Lagom's coffeeverse, customers can attend its regular cupping events.

The space may be minimalist in style but exudes warmth through playful artwork and friendly hospitality, which fosters a relaxed and sociable atmosphere. Nordic bakes and ciabatta sarnies fuel further fulfilment.

Established
2024

Key roastery
Fika Coffee Roasters

Brewing method
Espresso, filter, Orea

Machine
La Marzocco

Grinder
Mahlkonig E65S,
Mahlkonig EK43

Opening hours
Mon-Fri
8.30am-4.30pm
Sat-Sun
10am-4.30pm

(4) Sorcerer

Arch 4, Forth Street, Newcastle, Tyne and Wear, NE1 3NZ

sorcerercoffee

Opened in Newcastle city centre in 2021, Sorcerer is one of the few spots in the North East to serve delicious Dark Arts coffee. In March 2024, however, it paused for a radical refit and redirection.

Realising there was a gap in the market for a superior sandwich joint in the city, George Cummins of Sorcerer and Chris Coulter from Belly of the Beast decided to combine the magic of their respective businesses. The result of this alchemy is a new-look Sorcerer which combines Dark Arts espresso with a food menu inspired by traditional Italian-American style delis.

⚡ Spot touring artists who pop in before their gig at the Boiler Shop

Signature sub rolls are baked daily using Wildfarmed flour in the Belly of the Beast kitchens in Byker, before being whizzed over to Sorcerer to be enjoyed alongside an espresso or one of the consistent filters that are always ready as batch brew. Choose from a menu of solid classics such as the Deli Special: mortadella, salami, pepperoni and provolone cheese piled high and served with a crisp salad. Chase the savoury scran with a slice of lip-puckeringly zingy lemon meringue pie.

Dishes sell out quickly, especially on the weekend, so prebook via Instagram DM if you want to guarantee your pick of the day's menu.

Established
2021

Key roastery
Dark Arts Coffee

Brewing method
Espresso,
batch brew

Machine
La Marzocco Linea PB

Grinder
Mahlkonig E65S GbW,
Mahlkonig EK43 S

Opening hours
Tue-Fri
8am-3pm
Sat-Sun
10am-3pm

Newcastle

© Robert Steven

(5) Harvest

The city's pioneering speciality roastery, Ouseburn Coffee Co, serves the full spectrum of its own-roasted beans at this flagship cafe. The beautifully styled and airy spot demands a visit for recently roasted and well-prepped coffee paired with fresh and funky food.

91 St George's Terrace, Jesmond, Newcastle, NE2 2DN

ouseburncoffee.co.uk 🅞 ouseburncoffee 🎱

(7) Pink Lane Cafe

The cafe of the Pink Lane Coffee roastery, this spot opposite Central Station is the place to sample roasts sourced and bronzed by the Pink team. Work your way through the various espresso and pourover options then swerve the shakes by exploring the cafe menu of edibles.

1 Pink Lane, Newcastle, NE1 5DW

pinklanecoffee.co.uk

🅞 pinklanecoffeecollective

(6) Local NCL

It's ok to feel jealous that some people have this corner store as their local. Own-roasted and guest coffees, healthy food bowls, bakes, boutique ales and wines plus beans in bags are all on the menu. Happily, everyone's welcome — wherever they hail from. In summer, grab a table outdoors and make like a regular.

18 Acorn Road, Jesmond, Newcastle, NE2 2DJ

localncl.com 🅞 local_ncl

(8) Flat White Kitchen

This go-to brunch spot is in a cosy Grade-II listed building near the city's iconic castle and cathedral. The beans used are just as good as the location and sustainably sourced. Sweet treats are baked on-site daily and a brunch menu hums with feelgood food. Find its sister site on Elvet Bridge.

40 Saddler Street, Durham, DH1 3NU

flatwhitekitchen.com 🅞 flatwhitedurham 🎱

The Seahorse Coffee Box

Opposite The Green, The Front, Seaton Carew, Hartlepool, County Durham

theseahorsecoffeebox.co.uk | 07947 384408

theseahorsecoffeebox theseahorsecoffeebox

It isn't a trip to Seaton Carew without a stop at this coffee find on the seafront.

Don't be fooled into thinking you'd be unlikely to score a decent brew from a little horsebox though, as what The Seahorse lacks in size is made up for in its impressive coffee offering and talented baristas.

There are always two espressos available – one caffeinated and one decaf – which have been bronzed by the pros at Rounton Coffee Roasters. More unusually, quality drip coffee is also on the menu. It's a stellar choice for those who lean toward punchier flavours as it's made using a dark single-origin Brazilian roast. Lighter guest beans are a back-up option for those who like a filter with less intensity.

No judgement if you swap your coffee order for a warming cup of luxe hot chocolate

In the warmer months, beach bods go mad for the house cold brew. Founder Helen Gregory spent three years tinkering with her recipe, trialling different beans, brew times and kit to nail the perfect beach drink. All she'll share of the secret to mastering cold brew is that she uses a Toddy brewer, Great Taste award-winning beans and a trickle of naturally sweet oat milk.

The crew aren't afraid to flirt with coffee trends, so if you want to try a dalgona brew (whipped coffee) or biscoffee, this is the place to jump in.

Established
2020

Key roastery
Rounton Coffee Roasters

Brewing method
Espresso, drip, cold brew

Machine
Nuova Simonelli Appia Life

Grinder
Victoria Arduino Mythos One, Victoria Arduino MDJ, Eureka Mignon

Opening hours
Seasonal opening hours

Hartlepool

Mr Cooper's Coffee House – Bedford Street

27 Bedford Street, Middlesbrough, North Yorkshire, TS1 2LL

mrcoopersmiddlesbrough mrcooperscoffee_bedford.st

To celebrate five years of Mr Cooper's on Whitby's historic Church Street, the family team launched this sister store in Middlesbrough in 2023 which also revolves around the same MO of brews, bagels and beautiful things.

The extensive selection of alternative eats and treats begins at the counter, which bursts with bountiful bakes (we're looking at you, white choc and raspberry-stuffed Jammie Dodger cookie).

⚡ Hit up the merch selection stacked with prints, brewing kit, tees and reusable cups

The edibles extend to a seasonal bagel menu filled with unusual flavour combos, foraged items and homemade elements. Try the likes of oven-roasted courgette with miso glaze, rocket and homemade kimchi slaw. There are also colourful salads and grain bowls, plus natural wellness juices and shots.

The flavour journey isn't complete, of course, without the perfect pairing of a silky house espresso, courtesy of the Granary Blend from Rounton in Northallerton. Those who like a spot of flavour experimentation can scratch the itch with whatever's being showcased in the regular guest-roast spot. Roasteries that have recently hit the shelves include Spaceboy, Oddy Knocky, Radical Roasters, Hundred House and Round Hill.

Established
2023

Key roastery
Rounton Coffee Roasters

Brewing method
Espresso, V60, batch brew

Machine
La Marzocco Linea Classic

Grinder
Mahlkonig EK43, Mazzer Luigi

Opening hours
Mon-Sat
8am-3pm

Middlesbrough

(11) Scoundrels Coffee Co.

20 Station Street, Saltburn-by-the-Sea, North Yorkshire, TS12 1AE

scoundrelscoffee.co

f Scoundrels Coffee Co. ⊙ scoundrelscoffeeco

This eclectic Saltburn-by-the-Sea hangout enjoys the bragging rights of being the first coffee shop to bring speciality coffee and brewing methods beyond espresso to the town.

With its dizzying array of beans and serve styles, this is a great place for ditching your usual order and going off-piste. Liverpool's Crosby Coffee does the honours with the house beans while guest filter roasts are switched up regularly to showcase vivacious finds from the likes of Harmony Coffee Roaster in York. Sample the freshly brewed goods in the moodily lit inside space or head outdoors to the alfresco seating area to sip coffee in the fresh Saltburn-by-the-Sea air.

⏱ Visit between Wednesday and Sunday for the gourmet scotch egg

Pair your brew with something sweet from the huge selection of vegan baked goods, many of which feature an entire biscuit squished into the top of the bake. Cookie sandwiches are the house special and feature flavour combos like strawberry and pistachio, lemon and blueberry, and salted caramel.

Special events are frequent and varied at Scoundrels, a recent example was the afternoon where facial treatments (using a truffle skincare range) were paired with a brownie tasting plate and glass of fizz. True story. And, in deep midwinter, Father Christmas has been known to drop in to read to little ones while they devour hot chocolate and cookies.

Established
2023

Key roastery
Crosby Coffee
Roasters

Brewing method
Espresso, AeroPress,
V60, syphon,
cold brew

Machine
Nuova Simonelli
Appia Life

Grinder
Compak F8

Opening hours
Mon-Thu
8am-4pm
Fri-Sat
8am-5pm
Sun
9am-4pm

Saltburn-by-the-Sea

Mr Cooper's Coffee House – Church Street

72 Church Street, Whitby, North Yorkshire, YO22 4AS

01947 899904

 mrcooperswhitby mrcooperscoffee_church.st

There's little use trying to resist the baked delicacies at family-run Mr Cooper's, since the heaving cake curation is to be found on the counter from which you order coffee.

A silky espresso and a buttery bake is, of course, the ultimate union, and the cracking house blend, Granary, from Rounton Coffee Roasters in Northallerton delivers deliciously smooth and complementary chocolate-caramel notes. It's great black or with milk, and every cup is served with a mini Jammie Dodger.

To celebrate five years of Mr Cooper's, the team opened a new outpost in Middlesbrough

A regular showcase of guest beans extends the flavour possibilities for curious caffeine folk, and interesting roasts come from highly reputable roasteries such as Radical Roasters, Oddy Knocky, Round Hill, Hundred House and Spaceboy. Sample them as batch brew or V60.

For something savoury to counter the sweet carb-fest, explore the seasonal bagel menu. Creatively left-field fillings can be found in the likes of Argy Bhaji: onion bhaji, mango chutney, pink pickled onions, coconut, mint and cucumber raita, topped with poppadoms. Vibrant salads, grain bowls and wellness juices also feature – and all dishes are available to-go.

Don't forget to browse the in-store merch before leaving; it includes prints, brewing kits, tees and reusable cups.

Established
2018

Key roastery
Rounton Coffee Roasters

Brewing method
Espresso, V60, batch brew

Machine
Victoria Arduino Eagle One

Grinder
Mahlkonig EK43, Macap, Victoria Arduino Mythos Two

Opening hours
Mon-Sun
8am-4pm

Whitby

(13) Koda

17 Northway, Scarborough, North Yorkshire, YO11 1JH

f kodacoffeeshop ◎ koda.coffee

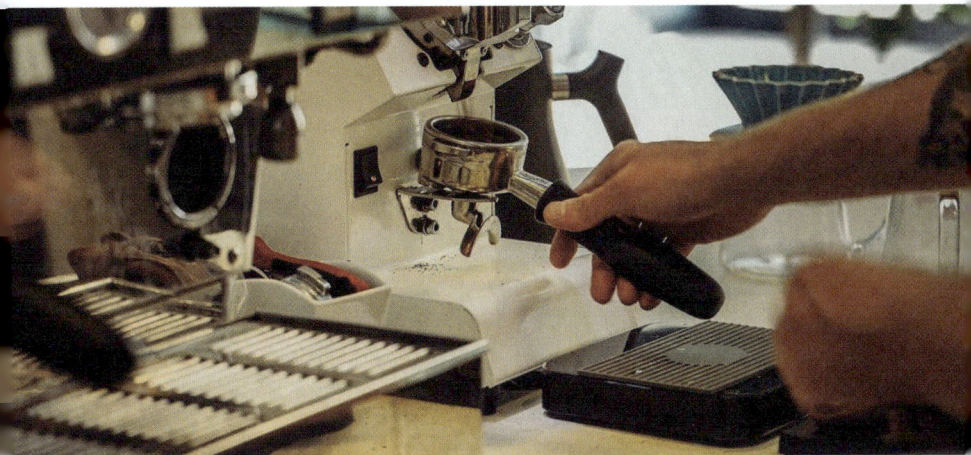

Koda's signature offering of six rotating coffees – one house, two guests, a house decaf, guest decaf and a syphon – has made it a speciality coffee must-visit in Scarborough.

Guest beans from global roasteries are switched up faster than shots can be knocked back, ensuring a visit always offers an exciting new brew to roadtest.

What's guaranteed is that one of the hoppers will be filled with the house espresso beans from hero roastery North Star. The Koda crew recently asked the roastery to source and develop an exclusive batch of beans to mark the fifth year of caffeinated collaboration between the two businesses. The result is a sweet and juicy washed Peruvian which delivers balanced notes of caramel, mandarin and apple.

☕ Hand brews and syphon coffees are served in beautiful custom cups from Potter & Clay

It's not just great tasting coffee that lures 'em in, however. The Koda team are also renowned for their warm welcome, banging playlists and plant-based creations such as umami-rich tempeh focaccia and kimcheese toasties.

Established
2019

Key roastery
North Star
Coffee Roasters

Brewing method
Espresso, pourover,
syphon

Machine
La Marzocco
Linea Classic

Grinder
Victoria Arduino
Mythos One,
Mahlkonig EK43

Opening hours
Mon-Sat
9am-5pm
Sun
10am-2pm

Scarborough

113

14 Roost Coffee – Espresso Bar

6 Talbot Yard, Yorkersgate, Malton, North Yorkshire, YO17 7FT

roostcoffee.co.uk | 01653 697635

roostcoffeeandroastery roost_coffee

BEEN THERE • BEEN THERE • BEEN THERE •

Yorkshire's foodie town of Malton was always going to need a kick-ass coffee establishment to satisfy the finely tuned palates of locals. Nearly a decade ago, Roost answered the call and founders Ruth and David opened not just an espresso bar and shop but also a small-batch roastery.

For a full-on flavour encounter, coincide your visit with Malton's monthly food market

The Espresso Bar is housed inside an 18th-century Grade II-listed carriage house (alongside five other artisan producers) and the building is now the inspiration behind the design of Roost's new packaging.

Relax on a slouchy leather sofa in a setting of exposed brick walls and industrial pipework and sip one of 12 single origins from countries such as Ecuador, Rwanda, India and Colombia. A Guatemalan Swiss Water Decaf is also available for those who've maxed out on caffeine.

Dogs are welcome at Roost, as are those who work from home and need the background whoosh of a steamer and the constant drip of top-notch coffee in order to crack on.

Make sure to nip into one of the neighbouring shops to stock up on artisan produce and goodies before heading home.

Established
2015

Key roastery
Roost Coffee

Brewing method
Espresso, pourover, batch brew

Machine
Rocket RE A

Grinder
Eureka Olympus 75E, Mahlkonig EK43, Rocket Faustino

Opening hours
Tue-Sat
9am-3pm

Malton

Kinship

97 Middle Street South, Driffield, East Yorkshire, YO25 6QE

kinshipcoffee.co.uk | 01377 272243

kinship.driffield kinship.coffee

The compact size of this market-town coffee shop didn't stop its founder from having big ambitions for its role in the local community.

When Tom Watson established Kinship in the centre of Driffield in September 2021, he chose a name that would reflect his aspiration to create a space where people from all walks of life could convene and connect over coffee.

As the only speciality venue within a 15-mile radius, this small space hums with activity. Coffee enthusiasts make the trip to get their fix of the house roast (Square Mile's Red Brick) and to sample the fortnightly changing guest roast, which often champions local roasteries such as Harmony in York.

⚡ Kinship recently got an alcohol licence – hit one of the Kinship Lates to celebrate

The venture has been so successful that it's proudly turned its customers into coffee snobs. Tom says: *'They tell me they no longer buy from national chains as they now know what good coffee tastes like. Their interest in the good stuff has been awakened.'* The intimate setting and no-gimmicks-just-great-coffee ethos has proved so popular there have been murmurings of expansion. However, Tom is resolved to keep things just as they are. He says: *'If we expanded, we might lose what makes Kinship, Kinship.'*

Established
2021

Key roastery
Square Mile
Coffee Roasters

Brewing method
Espresso, batch filter,
Clever Dripper

Machine
Victoria Arduino
Eagle One

Grinder
Mahlkonig E65
GbW x3,
Hey Cafe HC-880

Opening hours
Mon-Fri
8am-4pm
Sat
8am-2pm

Driffield

115

(16) **Rise — York**

44 Fossgate, York, Yorkshire, YO1 9TF

risebrunch.co.uk

⊙ risebrunch

© Tim Emmerton

The busy hub of Fossgate has drawn crowds to its community of indie shops and eateries for centuries, and in 2022 it welcomed another quality business to the street in the form of Rise.

The team's social-cafe concept has been brought to life since opening within this roomy spot, which is bathed in natural light. This outpost mirrors the original Rise in Preston and focuses on antipodean-style brunch dishes and espresso-based coffee from London's Ozone. The aesthetic is contemporary, fun and primed for the grid with its pastel-pink palette, bleached wood and hanging houseplants.

⏱ Pint-size pooches are welcome

An all-day menu is built around brunch classics such as eggs benedict, turkish eggs and açaí bowls, but elevated by the talented Rise chefs. Seasonal line-ups and specials keep the offering fresh; ogle the latest offerings, such as steak and eggs or mushroom flatbread, on the team's Instagram reels.

In summer, alfresco brunchers keen to soak up the Yorkshire sunshine pour out to the street seating. After brunching, grab a takeaway iced coffee or fresh smoothie and take a stroll around the city walls.

Established
2022

Key roastery
Ozone Coffee Roasters

Brewing method
Espresso

Machine
La Marzocco Linea PB

Grinder
Mahlkonig E65S

Opening hours
Mon-Fri
8am-5pm
Sat-Sun
9am-5pm

17 Heppni Bakeri

If luscious lamination is your jam, then this new bakeri in York is a must-visit. The quality of the handcrafted pastries is equalled only by the carefully prepped brews made with Cast Iron beans. The small space also hosts comedi evenings.

14 Swinegate, York, YO1 8AZ

heppnibakeri

18 Still

Formerly Two Gingers, this coffee shop's reincarnation as Still has grown its offering to one rooted in natural wines, well-crafted cocktails and flowers alongside high-grade speciality coffee. Keep an eye out for evening pop-ups.

21 Posterngate, Hull, East Yorkshire, HU1 2JN

stillposterngate.com still_posterngate

Number Thirteen

13 Castlegate, Knaresborough, North Yorkshire, HG5 8AR

numberthirteenknaresborough.co.uk | 01423 863058

🅵 thirteencastlegate 🅾 numberthirteenknaresborough

You may recognise Number Thirteen from the film *A Very British Christmas* but that isn't its only claim to fame as the cafe has also scooped a raft of awards since it opened in 2018. To date it's won the title of Sustainable Business Award three times and been voted Knaresborough's Favourite Coffee Shop for three years running.

Its founder Sarah Ward was inspired by Kiwi coffee culture during her stint backpacking and working in New Zealand, and decided to recreate the new-wave speciality scene in her native Yorkshire. As expected from a down-under-inspired cafe, the coffee is suitably top notch. Beans are supplied by local roastery Roost and supported by a monthly changing guest roast. Espresso may be the star serve, but ask nicely and you could get to sample the goods via V60.

ⓘ Number Thirteen has released two cookbooks – both are available to buy at the cafe

Sustainability is woven through the fabric of Number Thirteen and everything – from crockery to wallpaper – is preloved, upcycled or handmade. The result is a cafe sporting a unique vintage style. The same eco-conscious mindset is applied to the menu: locally sourced ingredients are used wherever possible and savoury treats are crafted by Harrogate's Manna Bakery. Even the milk arrives fresh in glass bottles from a local dairy.

Established
2018

Key roastery
Roost Coffee
& Roastery

Brewing method
Espresso, V60

Machine
Rocket Boxer

Grinder
Eureka Zenith 65S

Opening hours
Mon-Sat
9am-4pm

Knaresborough

(20) Bean Loved

17 Otley Street, Skipton, North Yorkshire, BD23 1DY

beanloved.co.uk | 01756 791534

f beanlovedskipton **◎** beanloved

Bean Loved has enjoyed over 17 years of cafe success, and its secret has been getting the basics right — which includes serving damn fine coffee.

Landscape, the bespoke house blend from Huddersfield's Dark Woods, turns newbies into returning regulars thanks to its subtle complexity and crowd-pleasingly sweet finish in espresso-based drinks. Guest roasts, including a lush decaf option from Northallerton's Rounton, receive equally rave reviews.

☕ Pick up beans roasted by Dark Woods and Rounton from the retail shelves

Another string to the cafe's bow are its top-notch breakfast, brunch and lunch menus. A talented crew of chefs make everything in-house and regularly update the offering to include fresh seasonal produce.

Lunch has been given an injection of street-food inspiration via the addition of bao buns and poke bowls, while brunch fans flock to Bean Loved for its sweet-potato fritter stack. This ever-popular choice features crispy fritters combined with roasted red pepper and onion, topped with a poached egg, smashed avo, grilled halloumi, homemade chilli jam and sriracha mayo.

An easy-going atmosphere and friendly baristas take the experience next-level.

Established
2007

Key roastery
Dark Woods Coffee

Brewing method
Espresso

Machine
La Marzocco KB90

Grinder
Mahlkonig E80,
Mahlkonig E65S

Opening hours
Mon-Fri
8am-3pm
Sat
8am-4pm
Sun
9am-3pm

Skipton

21 The Clubhouse

18 Newmarket Street, Skipton, North Yorkshire, BD23 2HR

theclubhousecc.co.uk

 theclubhousecc theclubhousecoffee

The Clubhouse has the flex of being the only cafe in Skipton serving own-roasted coffee. Kane Pulford-Roberts sources beans from across the globe and roasts them in small batches at his cafe's micro-roastery.

Now Kane and the team have added another notch to their belts by opening The Bakehouse, where resident baker Fliss North crafts carby goods each day for the cafe. Her plump honey maritozzi (Italian cream buns) are the perfect pairing for a syrupy espresso with steamed milk.

Regulars may notice a different look of late, as The Clubhouse has undergone a major rebrand which champions shop dog George (visiting pooches are also very welcome).

⊙ Check out after-dark treats like espresso martinis, and cheese and charcuterie boards

The cafe is the natural home of coffee enthusiasts, but it's also a popular hangout for Skipton's cycling community and runners, thanks to its Saturday morning run club. Cyclists, runners, and those simply taking a mid-morning break visit for coffee and toast with toppings like peanut butter, banana, seeds and honey to power them through the day.

Established
2018

Key roastery
The Clubhouse

Brewing method
Espresso,
batch brew,
AeroPress, V60,
Chemex

Machine
La Marzocco
Linea Classic

Grinder
Nuova Simonelli

Opening hours
Mon-Thu, Sat
8.30am-4pm
Fri
8.30am-8pm
Sun
10am-3pm

1 Stainburn Parade, Moortown, Leeds, West Yorkshire, LS17 6NA

rabbitholecoffee.co.uk

rabbithole.coffee

© Lou Wilcock

Born out of a desire to *make coffee without being pricks about it*, Rabbit Hole started life as a modest pop-up in which owner Ste Thomas would serve up great coffee and chat, come rain or shine.

In early 2021 his set-up moved from outside a pizza restaurant to Leeds' Harvey Nichols. Word soon spread about the banging brews – sans any speciality elitism – and it wasn't long before Ste ran with the momentum and launched this bricks-and-mortar joint at Stainburn Parade in Moortown, on the outskirts of the city.

Now working alongside Ste is a talented likeminded team who have generated a loyal following and a gorgeous community vibe thanks to their easygoing yet considered approach to coffee.

🐇 Student of Leeds Beckett University? Hit up Rabbit Hole's two new sites on City Campus

Demonstrating the dynamic spirit of collaboration in the coffee scene, the team work closely with Cuppers Choice, and have even learnt to roast the house beans themselves at the Sheffield roastery. A new (but already popular) tradition has also started, in which a barrel-aged version of the punchy house coffee is released at Christmastime.

A rotating guest coffee offers further flavour thrills, with the likes of Echelon and Campbell & Syme featuring regularly. Whichever serve style or bean you plump for, pair your pick with Rita's carrot cake which is handcrafted using a recipe from Ste's mum.

Established
2022

Key roastery
Cuppers Choice

Brewing method
Espresso, filter

Machine
Sanremo Café Racer

Grinder
Victoria Arduino
Mythos One

Opening hours
Mon-Sun
8am-4pm

Leeds

94 Otley Road, Far Headingley, Leeds, West Yorkshire, LS6 4BA

fikanorth.co.uk

f fikanorthcoffee fikanorth

Scandi coffee culture and the creative spirit of Yorkshire collide at this perma-cool coffee shop in Far Headingley.

Fika North's chilled space and thoughtful approach puts an emphasis on connection, encouraging visitors to slow down and enjoy the good things in life such as quality coffee and just-baked pastries and cakes.

☕ Coffee to-go? Swing by Fika North's new takeaway hatch

Since day dot the team have poured locally roasted coffee from Casa Espresso; its beans freshly ground in a duo of Mahlkonig grinders to be savoured as espresso. However, the baristas also rate batch brew and switch up the guest roast every week to showcase beans from the likes of Wales' Hard Lines, ensuring there's always something new and noteworthy to sample.

Massive toasted bagels are a staple on the savoury food menu and feature fillings such as halloumi with sweet-chilli jam, chilli flakes, crispy onion, pickles and greens. For a sweet hit, check out the winning selection of flaky pastries and springy cakes or, if your visit falls between April and September, the whippy ice cream.

Established
2019

Key roastery
Casa Espresso
Coffee Roasters

Brewing method
Espresso, batch brew

Machine
La Marzocco
Linea PB AV

Grinder
Mahlkonig EK43,
Mahlkonig E65 GbW

Opening hours
Mon-Fri
8am-5pm
Sat-Sun
9am-5pm

Leeds

54 Otley Road, Headingley, Leeds, West Yorkshire, LS6 2AL

thebowery.org | 01132 242284

bowleyleeds

A coffee shop, workspace and creative hub rolled into one, Bowery is a mecca for all things beautifully crafted – from perfectly poured Allpress espresso to art exhibitions.

The speciality coffee is curated by head barista Ged Togher, who not only dispatches exceptional espresso and filter coffee but also shares his bean boffinry with budding baristas at the regular Bowery Coffee School workshops.

Sip a flat white in Bowery's 'secret garden'

Those visiting for a brew can chase the caffeine buzz with a sugar hit from the cafe's array of alluring bakes, before settling down to immerse themselves in the ambience. For more substantial eats, a line-up of hearty toasted sandwiches and vibrant salads delivers big-time.

Bowery is as much a creative space as a coffee shop, thanks to its art gallery and regular calendar of exhibitions, workshops and short courses (soap making, watercolour painting and creative writing have all featured), as well as events and parties. It's freelancer-friendly too and has a dedicated workspace so laptop warriors can feel free to plug in and blast through their inbox as they work through the drinks menu.

Established
2008

Key roastery
Allpress Espresso

Brewing method
Espresso, filter

Machine
La Marzocco
Linea Classic

Grinder
Mazzer Super Jolly

Opening hours
Mon-Sun
9am-5pm

Leeds

25 Coffee On The Crescent

2 The Crescent, Hyde Park, Leeds, West Yorkshire, LS6 2NW

coffeeonthecrescent.co.uk | 01132 160380

f coffeeonthecrescentleeds **◎** coffeeonthecrescent

The combination of community vibes and spectacular speciality coffee make this Hyde Park hangout stand out from the crowd.

Ex-professional cricketer and self-confessed coffee geek Timothy Linley launched Coffee on the Crescent in 2017, envisioning it as a place where Leeds folk could come together to escape, relax and connect over coffee.

Rather than committing to one roastery, Tim's team of experienced baristas rotate the coffee offering, sourcing the goods from multiple celebrated roasteries. Consequently, the menu is always changing and showcases multiple regions, processing methods, tasting profiles and brewing methods.

Want to switch up your usual espresso order to a V60? COTC is the place to do it. Need some home brewing advice? The friendly baristas are always happy to share their tricks of the trade.

☕ COTC's almond croissants and cinnamon buns are legendary

The brunch offering matches the quality of the coffee being served. Avocado-topped toast, homemade toasties and seeded ciabatta rolls stuffed with seasonal fillings ensure visitors leave well-fed as well as expertly caffeinated.

Established
2017

Key roastery
Multiple roasteries

Brewing method
Espresso, V60,
batch filter

Machine
La Marzocco Linea

Grinder
Fiorenzato F64 EVO

Opening hours
Mon-Fri
8am-4.30pm
Sat
8.30am-4.30pm
Sun
9am-4.30pm

Leeds

26 Stage Espresso & Brew Bar

41 Great George Street, Leeds, West Yorkshire, LS1 3BB

stagecoffee.com

f stagecoffee 🔘 stagecoffeeleeds

Stage debuted on the Leeds coffee scene in 2017 and remains firmly in the limelight.

The team at this coffee shop don't do things by halves so they garner rave reviews for everything from bean sourcing to brew style and service. Rather than sticking to a house coffee or specific roaster, they've plumped for single-estate beans from a bill of hero roasteries (Echelon, Chipp, Maude and North Star all feature) which take turns to own the stage when showcased via the La Marzocco, batch brew or Clever Dripper.

⚡ Ditch your usual coffee order for one of the seasonal specials – the maple and cinnamon latte was a previous fan fave

A counter laden with locally made bakes form a supporting cast to the speciality brews. Pastries arrive freshly baked each morning from Harrogate's Bakeri Baltzersen and, while its almond croissant is a routine bestseller, there's something glorious about dipping a classic croissant in a silky smooth coffee.

Once caffeinated, check out the humongous range of coffee kit on the retail shelves – including every type of filter paper you could ever need – together with a range of regularly changing coffees.

Beyond the daytime scoffing and slurping are evening workshops and special events. Local craft beers, wines, artisan soft drinks and late-night espressos fuel the after-hours fun.

Established
2017

Key roastery
Multiple roasteries

Brewing method
Espresso,
batch brew, cold brew

Machine
La Marzocco GB5 S

Grinder
Victoria Arduino
MYG85,
Mahlkonig EK43

Opening hours
Mon-Fri
8am-3.30pm
(seasonal opening hours)

Leeds

125

27 Kapow Coffee

15 Thornton's Arcade, Leeds, West Yorkshire, LS1 6LQ

kapowcoffee.co.uk | 07480 132204

kapowcoffee

This colourful comic-book-inspired coffee shop within Leeds' Thornton's Arcade is home to some of the city's most experienced baristas.

The team's fanaticism for all things speciality is immediately obvious from their comprehensive retail offering, which is one of the best in Yorkshire. Beans from Kawa, Friedhats, Assembly, New Ground and many more regularly boss the shelves. A plethora of brewing equipment is also available to help visitors make the most of their pick of the beans on sale, while clued-up and friendly baristas are on hand with brewing advice.

🔵 Check out the art space showcasing the work of local creatives

Kapow's own custom blend of naturally processed Brazilian and Ethiopian beans – roasted by one of the team at local roastery Chipp Coffee Co. – is the main house coffee and the crew go the extra mile to ensure every shot is spot on. Even if you're just popping in to pick up a bag of beans, it would be madness to leave without grabbing a flattie for the road.

The Kapow coffee team share their geekery further via an expanding events calendar, which includes the likes of cuppings, competitions and tastings. Keep an eye on socials for the latest.

Established
2013

Key roastery
Kapow Coffee

Brewing method
Espresso, batch filter, pourover

Machine
Sanremo Opera 2.0

Grinder
Mahlkonig E65 GbW x2, Mahlkonig EK43, Weber Workshops Key, Ceado E5SD

Opening hours
Mon-Fri
7.30am-6pm
Sat
8am-6pm
Sun
10am-4.30pm

(28) Laynes

12-16 New Station Street, Leeds, West Yorkshire, LS1 5DL

laynescafe.co.uk | 07828 823189

laynescafe

Located just a minute's walk from Leeds railway station is one of the city's speciality coffee institutions. It's a must-visit, even if just for a fly-by brew to-go.

What started in 2011 as a pioneering espresso bar has enjoyed an extension into the unit next door, the launch of a sister bakery, and the implementation of later opening hours for wining and dining. Through these activities, founder Dave Olejnik has turned Laynes into a dynamic destination for discerning coffee lovers.

While the hotspot now attracts as many visitors for its bougie all-day brunch plates as it does for its espresso, the focus on serving the finest speciality coffee hasn't wavered. Its skilled baristas enjoy the rep of pouring some of the best flat whites in the city.

Laynes' bold yellow exterior and patterned brew-bar tiles make this one for your Insta grid

A daytime trip to Laynes could see you sipping a single-origin Square Mile coffee and feasting on the likes of turkish eggs comprising poachies, halloumi, flatbread, spinach, garlic yogurt, and sage and chilli butter. However, come 5pm, brews and brunches are swapped for cocktails and multi-course meals: think beef short-rib ragu with soft polenta, sage and pecorino, chased by a sticky date pudding paired with a Cold Fashioned (whisky, cold-brew liqueur and cocoa bitters).

Established
2011

Key roastery
Square Mile
Coffee Roasters

Brewing method
Espresso, batch brew

Machine
Synesso MVP

Grinder
Mahlkonig E80,
Mahlkonig E65S GbW,
Mahlkonig EK43

Opening hours
Mon-Wed
7.30am-9pm
Thu-Fri
7.30am-10pm
Sat
8am-10pm
Sun
9am-4pm

(29) Archive

94 Kirkstall Road, Leeds, West Yorkshire, LS3 1HD

archiveleeds.co.uk | 07444 710139

 archiveleeds archiveleeds

It's only natural that this coffee shop and events space within Prime Studios – one of the largest independent film and television studios in the north of England – has found fame for its crowd-pleasing food and drinks. While star-studded dramas are being filmed in the surrounding studios, Archive turns out its own works of art in the form of rosetta-adorned lattes and pap-worthy brunch and lunch plates.

Planning a mega knees-up? Archive can hold 250 for private parties

An exciting menu of edibles features classic cafe fare like smashed avo on toast and eggs benny, alongside newer favourites such as shakshuka topped with za'atar and tarragon, served with buttered sourdough toast.

On the coffee front, star billing goes to the house espresso from Casa which is fabulous as a velvety flat white. Alternatively, choose from a supporting cast of guest pourovers from the likes of Hard Lines, Echelon, Dark Arts and Square Mile.

Local? Check out Archive's regular events, which range from film screenings and vintage-clothing pop-ups to live music and board-game nights. The team recently upped the ante for their events by installing a new Funktion-One sound system and lighting rig.

Established
2019

Key roastery
Casa Espresso

Brewing method
Espresso, filter, cold brew

Machine
Victoria Arduino Eagle One

Grinder
Mahlkonig E65S GbW

Opening hours
Mon-Wed
9am-3pm
Thu
9am-9pm
Sat-Sun
10am-4pm
(check socials for evening events)

(30) Galleria

Project House, Armley Road, Leeds, West Yorkshire, LS12 2DR

galleria-lds.com | 01138 214029

☉ galleria_lds

It was only a matter of time before a fly coffee bar appeared in the heart of Leeds' new cultural concept, Project Households. Find it, canalside, on the edge of the city centre.

While the wood-fired flatbreads served morning, noon and night are pretty special, it's the speciality single-origin espresso and batch brew that send out the bat signal to caffeine addicts across the city.

Local roastery North Star provides the house and decaf espresso, changing up the house blend quarterly to shine a spotlight on beans from different farms and keep things seasonal. Galleria's batch-brew selection and retail beans hail from various roasteries across the UK, including Oddkin, Origin, Curve and Outpost, as well as those closer to home like Chipp Coffee Co. and Echelon.

⚡ Keep an eye on socials for news of gigs, food markets and free yoga sessions

Galleria's reputation continues to grow and, coffee aside, it also provides tasty pre-gig snacks for those visiting the 1,000-capacity event space where the likes of Idles, Royal Blood, Ezra Collective, Floating Points and Nightmares On Wax have all played.

Established
2024

Key roastery
North Star
Coffee Roasters

Brewing method
Espresso, batch brew, cold brew

Machine
La Marzocco
Linea Classic S

Grinder
Fiorenzato F64 EVO,
Eureka Mignon,
Hey Cafe HC-880

Opening hours
Mon-Wed
9am-3pm
Thu-Sat
9am-11pm
Sun
10am-3pm

Leeds

129

31 The Hideout @ Harper Farm

Harper Farm, Whitehall Road, Leeds, West Yorkshire, LS12 6JU

harperfarm.co.uk

 harperhideout harperhideout

© Lynsey Doran

A ten-minute drive is all that separates Leeds locals from the pleasures of caffeine, cruffins and cute livestock on Harper Farm.

In 2023 the family-run team opened the doors to The Hideout, a charming cafe housed in what used to be the farm's red-brick dairy. The refurbed space now channels contemporary cafe styling, framed by a duck-egg brew bar of elite coffee kit and bags of speciality coffee. However, The Hideout remains happily in keeping with its rural setting through rustic wooden beams, benches and sink-in-able leather sofas.

Lusciously smooth espresso is churned out by friendly baristas who enlist the help of Dark Woods to keep the grinders topped up with seasonal beans. These precious goods form a small but on-point menu of espresso drinks, which is complemented by a selection of daily changing fresh bakes, weekend specials, sausage rolls and savoury scones. Have a snoop of The Hideout's socials to find out what's fresh on the menu.

🛈 Electric car low on juice?
Plug in at one of the EV charging points

The experience is made even sweeter by the view of Gary the llama and a herd of goats (known to regulars as Gary and the gang) playing in the fields. If they're not in view from the cafe, scout them out for a post-coffee pick-me-up (of the less caffeinated variety).

Established
2023

Key roastery
Dark Woods Coffee

Brewing method
Espresso

Machine
La Marzocco
Linea Classic S

Grinder
Anfim Pratica

Opening hours
Mon-Sun
10am-4pm

Leeds

130

32 Moi Outside

Unit 2 New Oxford House, Albert Street, Hebden Bridge,
West Yorkshire, HX7 8AH

moi-outside.com 🔲 moi_outside

This Hebden Bridge coffee shop and retailer is a great find for attention-grabbing drinks and warm community vibes in the soul of the South Pennines. Outdoorsy types, coffee lovers and those after somewhere comfy to chill while scoffing delicious bites carve out time to visit and convene over well-crafted brews.

The calibre of the coffee and extensive bean offering is superb: North Star's The Docks – a chocolatey and nutty blend with a buttery body – gets top-dog status as the house espresso, while batch brew is rotated bi-weekly to showcase experimental roasts.

⚡ Hit the trails with like-minded folk at Moi Outside's social run club, Pathfinder

The team favour new-wave and fruit-forward omni roasts, so the retail shelves heave with bags of flavour-bomb beans from the likes of Scenery Coffee Roasters, A.M.O.C, Red Bank, Casa Espresso and Origin.

The crew's brewing skills and knowledge may be as high grade as those speciality beans, yet the coffee experience is pleasingly down to earth. Coffees are often described using childhood sweets as reference points instead of inaccessible coffee descriptions.

And if motivation or reward are needed to join one of the cafe's social runs, then sourdough cinnamon-sugar donuts, iced orbs and Schlossberger gruyère grilled cheese are guaranteed to do the trick.

Established
2022

Key roastery
North Star
Coffee Roasters

Brewing method
Espresso, batch filter,
cold brew

Machine
La Marzocco
Linea Classic

Grinder
Mahlkonig EK43,
Fiorenzato F64 EVO

Opening hours
Wed-Thu
8am-3pm
Fri
8am-4pm
Sat
9am-4pm
Sun
10am-3pm

Hebden Bridge

131

Unit 3a Copley Business Park, Wakefield Road, Halifax, West Yorkshire, HX3 0UA

thebakeryhalifax.co.uk

thebakerycopley

This family-run venue has a no-compromise MO: to support and promote local producers in every way possible. The artisan bread used in the sarnies, the fresh milk steamed for flat whites, the coffee beans used and the indulgent slabs of cake adorning the counter are all made, produced, roasted or crafted within shouting distance, if not in-house.

🎯 Yield to the temptation of the local bakes on the countertop

For the coffee, it wouldn't be possible to find beans roasted more locally than Halifax's White Rose Coffee Roasters, just five minutes away. The roastery has created a house blend unique to The Bakery, which is made using Brazilian beans (grown at 1,200m by a fifth-generation farmer at Fazenda Inhame in Campos Altos) and Indian Monsoon Malabar beans. The latter are processed by exposure to monsoon rain and winds for three to four months before being harvested post-monsoon as plump, mature beans. Medium roasting results in a coffee with well-rounded body and a strong hint of spice – perfect as espresso or paired with fresh local milk.

Local businesses are celebrated and guest roasts also feature, a recent example being a batch from Huddersfield's celebrated Dark Woods.

Established
2020

Key roastery
White Rose
Coffee Roasters

Brewing method
Espresso, V60

Machine
La Marzocco
Linea Classic S

Grinder
Fiorenzato F64 EVO

Opening hours
Mon-Sun
8.30am-4.30pm

Halifax

132

(34) Arcade Coffee & Food

9-10 Byram Arcade, Huddersfield, West Yorkshire, HD1 1ND
arcadecoffee.co.uk | 01484 511148

 arcadecoffeefood arcadecoffeefood

© David Fulford

Housed in a grand Victorian arcade, this Huddersfield fave is a dynamite find for those in search of speciality coffee and delicious food.

It's a popular spot for recaffeination after a wander through the indie shops of Byram Arcade — the encaustic-tiled floors and atrium seating providing a pleasingly historic counterpoint to Arcade's on-trend playlist and relaxed vibe.

Dark Woods Coffee, just seven miles away, roasts the beans for the cafe's reliably good house espresso, while guest roasts are available on batch and cold brew.

🔵 Sign up to take part in the monthly small-plates supper club

It would be remiss to skip the all-day brunch menu when visiting, as vibrant dishes like kimchi hash browns, turkish eggs and ricotta doughnuts feature. There's also a cheerful selection of lunchtime bagels and daily specials.

The Arcade crew switch up both the brunch and coffee menus seasonally, and have even ramped up their small-plates evening set-up to include wine pairings and bespoke cocktails. On Sundays, the Arcade chefs turn their attention to delivering mighty roast dinners.

A schedule of events runs throughout the week and includes live experimental music, book launches and queer book pop-ups.

Established
2017

Key roastery
Dark Woods Coffee

Brewing method
Espresso,
batch brew,
cold brew

Machine
La Marzocco
Linea Classic

Grinder
Anfim Pratica

Opening hours
Mon-Sat
8am-4.30pm
Sun
10am-4pm

Huddersfield

35　Coffeevolution

8 Church Street, Huddersfield, West Yorkshire, HD1 1DD
coffeevolution.co.uk | 01484 432881

 coffeevolution coffeevolutionhuddersfield

Coffeevolution recently celebrated being at the helm of Huddersfield's speciality coffee scene for a quarter of a century.

Considered an institution in local circles, the coffee shop is still owned by the same family who originally brought third-wave coffee culture to the Yorkshire town. The Perkins brothers (who also own roastery Bean Brothers Coffee Company) keep their fingers on the pulse on the ever-changing coffee scene, ensuring the beans they roast and brew methods they utilise are in line with contemporary palates. Ask the baristas what's currently firing up the roastery team and you might even get to sample an experimental batch of something fresh and funky.

🛈 Snoop the retail shelves for own-roasted beans, coffee kit and vintage brewing ephemera

Meeting the needs of modern customers extends to the cafe's wider drinks offering and Coffeevolution recently increased its range of craft beers and ciders. It also updated and expanded its outdoor seating area and introduced longer opening hours. The result is an increase in post-work visitors swinging by for artisan libations in the late-afternoon sun.

Coffeevolution's comforting food menu showcases regulars' favourites, like its bacon and cream-cheese bagel and grilled sourdough sarnies, alongside an alluring selection of cakes and pastries.

Established
2000

Key roastery
Bean Brothers
Coffee Company

Brewing method
Espresso, V60,
Chemex, AeroPress,
cold brew

Machine
La Marzocco FB80

Grinder
Mahlkonig K30 Twin,
Mahlkonig EK43

Opening hours
Mon-Fri
7am-6pm
Sat
7.30am-5pm
Sun
9am-4pm

Huddersfield

36 Espresso Corner

11 Kirkgate, Huddersfield, West Yorkshire, HD1 1QS

espressocorner.co.uk | 01484 427325

espressocorner ⃝ espressocorner

BEEN THERE · BEEN THERE · BEEN THERE · BEEN THERE

One of the best-rated cafes in Huddersfield, Espresso Corner is celebrated for its winning combination of comfy styling, artisanal bites and shameless coffee geekery.

Soft music, lively chatter and the aroma of freshly ground Square Mile and Bean Brothers coffees waft across a room neatly scattered with vintage school desks, wooden benches and verdant plants. On entry, it's hard not to be distracted by the retro bike hanging on the wall, but the scents drifting from the La Marzocco machine soon lure customers to the counter.

Whether brewed using the house beans (Square Mile's silky Red Brick blend) or the guest offering (an Ethiopian, Brazilian and El Salvadorian blend care of Bean Brothers' Derek), coffee is served with slick precision. If you're lucky your brew may be served in a bespoke ceramic cup, thanks to a recent collab with local potter Phil Russell.

🕐 Take your coffee outside and sip it in the new alfresco seating area

A selection of bakes entice from the countertop, and it's near impossible to resist carby creations such as lemon and pistachio blondie, cinnamon buns and raspberry-cheesecake brownies.

For savoury treats, look no further than freshly crafted sandwiches made with bread from Roger's Bakery, or breakfast staples like the classic bacon sandwich or avo on toast with feta and lime.

Established
2013

Key roastery
Square Mile
Coffee Roasters

Brewing method
Espresso, V60,
AeroPress, syphon,
Chemex

Machine
La Marzocco Linea PB

Grinder
Mahlkonig K30 Twin,
Mazzer, Anfim

Opening hours
Mon-Fri
8am-5pm
Sat
8am-4pm

Huddersfield

Peel St. Social

1 Peel Street, Marsden, West Yorkshire, HD7 6BR

01484 963640

 peelstsocial peelstsocial

Ste Fulton and Blyth Little may have opened Peel St. Social just over a year ago but, in that short time, they've cultivated a vibrant and bustling hub in the village of Marsden. It's all down to the pair's uber-welcoming attitude, cracking coffee, seasonal menus, sell-out Sunday roasts and events like creative socials and jazz festivals.

The Peel St. crew are proud pourers of Dark Woods, whose beans are roasted a mere mile away. House blend Driftwood is a Colombian brew featuring notes of caramel, almond and stone fruit: a sweet combo when paired with milk but equally delicious black. Fix a return visit to explore its supporting cast of cherry blossom matcha and craft beers (on tap), then ogle the retail shelves to pimp your home brew bar with beans from the likes of Warminster's Girls Who Grind, Ride & Grind in Edinburgh and Cardiff's Hard Lines.

💧 Arrive early to bag a sheltered balcony seat with views of the village

The food offering is as carefully curated as the caffeine hits and reflects the bountiful produce to be found in the village and surrounds. The meat is butchered locally, with sausages (regular and merguez) made by a farm within shouting distance. Coffee and dairy products are all ultra local. The Handmade Bakery supplies all the bread, and cakes are all baked in-house (the legendary bakewell blondie is a must-try).

Established
2023

Key roastery
Dark Woods Coffee

Brewing method
Espresso, cold brew

Machine
Sanremo Zoe Compact

Grinder
Anfim Milano, Anfim Pratica

Opening hours
Tue-Wed
10am-8pm
Thu
10am-10pm
Fri-Sat
10am-11pm
Sun
10am-7pm

Marsden

(38) Wired Coffee and Cake

17 Church Street, Honley, Holmfirth, Yorkshire, HD9 6AH

07598 931448

 wiredcoffeeandcake wiredcoffeeandcake

© Shaun Flannery

Crunchy rocky road, chewy flapjack, gooey brownies and lemon and blackcurrant curd cake are just a slice of the house-baked thrills to be scoffed at this Honley hub of coffee and cake.

Wired's team of flavoursmiths — headed up by SCA professional barista (and La Marzocco Barista Hero finalist 2024) Oliver Schofield and his business partner and wife Katie Schofield — pair their delicious homemade bakes with the juicy-fruit flavours and vibrant sweet notes of house blends from local roastery Dark Woods. These are made bespoke for Wired, and change every quarter. Those seeking an off-piste coffee and cake experience will discover an assortment of flavours in rotating guest roasts from the UK, USA and Europe (available via V60 and Clever Dripper).

While the lip-smacking bakes and brews take centre stage, there is a cracking selection of savoury brunch dishes worth exploring, too.

🕒 Join the regular Wired Walk meet-ups for soul-nourishing stomps in good company

Following a generous feed and caffeine fix, be sure to have a snoop around the retail selection which features a collection of preserves, honeys and hot choc, as well as an assortment of speciality-grade coffee for next-level home brews.

Established
2018

Key roastery
Dark Woods Coffee

Brewing method
Espresso, V60,
Clever Dripper

Machine
La Marzocco Linea PB

Grinder
Mahlkonig K30

Opening hours
Fri-Sat
9.30am-3pm
Sun
10am-3pm

Holmfirth

137

39 Danelaw Coffee

Holmfirth Filling Station, 236 Huddersfield Road, Holmfirth,
West Yorkshire, HD9 3TT

danelaw.coffee | 07506 900331 | f danelawcoffee danelawcoffee.thongsbridge

Fresh on the cafe scene — although not the northern coffee scene — is
Danelaw Coffee. Those in the know will be familiar with David Jameson's
Danelaw espresso, decaf and single-origin roasts which have all bagged
awards since the roaster launched in 2022. Things have gone so well that
the coffee operation has now expanded to include this cafe space.

The new site is housed at a petrol station forecourt ('I can't tell if it's
genius or insanity, but it's somewhere in that zone,' says David) and deals
in delicious espresso drinks and seasonal batch brew, as well as selling
own-roasted beans to-go.

Pair an own-roasted flat white with a sticky cinnamon bun

The coffee is, of course, largely made using Danelaw roasts but David does
occasionally bring in guest beans when the coffee helps towards a good
cause or is particularly exceptional, such as a recent showcasing of local
roaster Yellow Bear. Quality brews, plus the cafe's dog-friendly status and
free parking (hard to come by in Holmfirth) have made it a great success.

It's now Holmfirth's grab-and-go coffee stop, the only short delays
resulting from customers stopping to take a selfie with the cafe's
custom GB5 espresso machine.

Established
2024

Key roastery
Danelaw Coffee

Brewing method
Espresso, batch brew

Machine
La Marzocco GB5

Grinder
La Marzocco Swan,
Mazzer Super Jolly

Opening hours
Mon-Fri
6.30am-4pm
Sat-Sun
8am-3pm

Holmfirth

40 Old George Coffee House – Market Hill

14 Market Hill, Barnsley, South Yorkshire, S70 2QE

old-george.co.uk | 01226 695700

 oldgeorgebarn oldgeorgebarnsley

Roll back to 2010 when something special happened in South Yorkshire: Gareth Derbyshire and Andrew McCulloch met and dreamt up a plan for a better life. This dream involved (after endless traipsing to Sheffield and Leeds in search of a decent brew) opening a coffee shop. Seven years later the dream became reality and today they have four coffee houses to their name: two in Barnsley and one each in Sheffield and Huddersfield.

Customers rave about the next-level coffee, attentive front-of-house team and banging brunches at the pair's Barnsley cafe. It's been such a success that it pays to arrive early on weekends to bag a table.

The house blend – a dark-roasted Peruvian and Colombian combo packing a chocolate and treacle punch – hails from their good friends at Foundation Coffee in St Ives. The single-origin option, Q'antxabina from Guatemala, is a fruitier affair with notes of green apple, plum, chocolate and hazelnut.

For further caffeine kicks, check out Old George's little bro at Town Hall

Brunchtime visitors can enjoy sweet thrills such as pancake stacks with Biscoff and strawberries, or get stuck into the full gamut of traditional brekkie faves such as eggs benny and breakfast sandwiches stuffed with fried eggs and sausages. Furry friends are welcome and even have their own menu, which includes puppuccinos and doggy sausages.

Established
2017

Key roastery
Foundation Coffee Roasters

Brewing method
Espresso, V60, AeroPress, filter

Machine
Faema E71

Grinder
Mahlkonig E80 GbW

Opening hours
Mon-Sun
9am-4pm

Barnsley

Holme Coffee House

3 High Street, Penistone, Sheffield, South Yorkshire, S36 6BR

holmecoffeehouse.co.uk | 01226 445990

holmecoffeehouse

BEEN THERE · BEEN THERE · BEEN THERE ·

Fans of Holme's original brunch hotspot in Holmfirth should be doing cartwheels. The OG has been so loved since it opened in 2019 that the team had the confidence to fling open the doors of this sister site in Penistone. They've brought the good coffee, food and chilled vibes with them and are feeding and watering – among others – walkers making a pitstop on the Trans Pennine Trail. Happily, brunch is an all-day, seven-days-a-week affair at Holme.

🛈 Try the house-fave french toast with its seasonally switched-up toppings

Complementing the coffee shop's funky interiors, sweet-as playlists and smiley service is a range of locally roasted artisan coffee from Bean Brothers in nearby Huddersfield. Guest coffees also feature, sourced from roasteries including Elsewhere Coffee, Radical, Sanctuary and Oddy Knocky.

Don't worry about booking as, in laidback style, this spot operates on a walk-in only basis. Rock up and the team will get you seated and sorted with something epic from the fresh and seasonal menu.

Established
2023

Key roastery
Bean Brothers
Coffee Company

Brewing method
Espresso, V60

Machine
La Marzocco
Linea Classic

Grinder
Mahlkonig E65S GbW

Opening hours
Mon-Sat
9am-4pm
Sun
9.30am-4pm

42 Old George Coffee House – Fox Valley

Unit B5 Fox Valley, Stocksbridge, Sheffield, South Yorkshire, S36 2AB

old-george.co.uk | 01143 089411

Old George Fox Valley oldgeorgefoxvalley

Barnsley's original coffee hotspot is now serving up its trademark chilled vibes and brew-tiful moments in the swanky new Fox Valley complex – a 28-acre former steelworks site in north Sheffield which has undergone a £50m redevelopment.

With a team of experienced baristas, chefs and front-of-house staff showcasing epic talent – from brewing the perfect cup to pouring incredible latte art and crafting great food – the team are 100 per cent dedicated to the good things in life.

Fantasy of becoming a barista? Book onto one of the Old George courses

This may be the brand's fourth site (there are two in Barnsley and another in Huddersfield) but the team pride themselves on creating the same high standard of coffee and food in each of the Old George outlets.

Visit for a warm welcome, a caffeine buzz and feelgood sweet treats: take comfort in a bounty of brownies, blondies and other traybakes on the cake counter while sinking a brew from main bean supplier Foundation.

Established
2024

Key roastery
Foundation
Coffee Roasters

Brewing method
Espresso, V60,
batch brew

Machine
Victoria Arduino
Eagle One

Grinder
Mahlkonig E80 GbW

Opening hours
Mon-Sun
9am-4pm

(43) Albie's Coffee

22 Snig Hill, Sheffield, South Yorkshire, S3 8NB

f albiessheffield albiessheffield

With its glass frontage, bright and airy interior and leafy green foliage, this coffee shop in Sheffield's legal district is an inviting find for caffeinated respite away from the urban bustle.

Commuters, professionals and locals routinely drop in to savour a cup of expertly crafted coffee, choosing to grab a seat by the window to watch the world go by as they sip or soak up sunny rays at one of the outdoor tables.

Check out sister venue NinetyFour in Chesterfield

Albie's house coffee comes courtesy of local roastery Cuppers Choice. The partnership not only guarantees freshness but also minimises waste, as the coffee is delivered in reusable 4kg tubs instead of disposable packaging. A different guest roastery takes the spotlight each month – past favourites have included Artisan Roast, Oddy Knocky and Hard Lines.

A small but thoughtfully curated food menu features the likes of bagels loaded with pulled chicken, hot sauce and pickles, and indulgent french toast topped with streaky bacon and showered with maple syrup. The cafe's signature banana bread, baked fresh daily, is delicious down to the last crumb.

Established
2018

Key roastery
Cuppers Choice

Brewing method
Espresso,
Moccamaster

Machine
La Marzocco

Grinder
Anfim, Mazzer,
Mahlkonig EK43

Opening hours
Mon-Fri
8am-4pm

Sheffield

(44) Mow's Coffee

151 Arundel Street, Sheffield, South Yorkshire, S1 2NU

themowbray.co.uk/the-mowbray-cafe

coffeeatmows

This stylish caffeine den on Sheffield's Arundel Street has its priorities in order: coffee first, everything else second.

East London roastery Dark Arts Coffee supplies the seasonally changing house espresso, while guest roasts are sourced from esteemed global roasteries such as Berlin's The Barn, Onyx Coffee Lab in Arkansas and Rotterdam's A Matter of Concrete.

The gang source in small batches so the coffee and the menu are always fresh. Mow's baristas are a dab hand at extracting every ounce of flavour from those beans, whether as shots for a flat white or clean filter brews. The seasonal drink specials are also worth exploring and have included creative concoctions such as lavender and rosemary white-chocolate mocha.

Mow's laidback 'eat-at-any-time' ethos comes from the belief that the food you really fancy should be eaten whenever the heck you want it. If that means kickstarting the day with a grilled cheese toastie of monterey jack cheddar and Depot Bakery sourdough, chased by a slab of cake, so be it.

In a hurry? Grab a cortado and pain au chocolat to-go from the takeaway hatch

The best spot in the house for perching while sipping your pick of the coffee menu is at the custom-made espresso bar, which has been crafted from antique marble and reclaimed timber.

Established
2020

Key roastery
Dark Arts Coffee

Brewing method
Espresso, filter

Machine
Sanremo Cafe Racer

Grinder
Mahlkonig E80,
Mahlkonig E65S,
Compak PK100

Opening hours
Mon-Fri
8am-5pm
Sat
9am-5pm
Sun
9am-4pm

Sheffield

Tamper Coffee Sellers Wheel

45 Old George Coffee House – Huddersfield

When, in 2010, Old George owners Garath and Andrew packed in their day jobs to open a coffee shop they had no idea that one day they'd be running a mini empire of four indie coffee shops, including this lovely Huddersfield cafe. Find its siblings in Barnsley and Sheffield.

Heritage Mills, 70 Plover Road, Lindley, Huddersfield, HD3 3HR

old-george.co.uk ◎ oldgeorgebarnsley ⅋

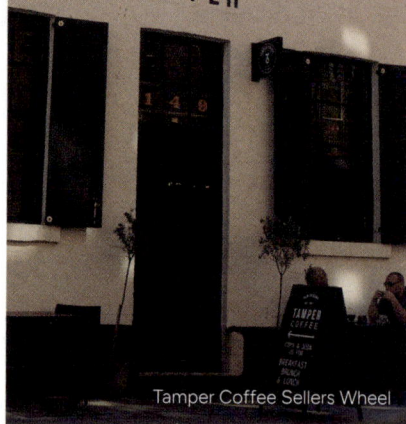

46 Depot Bakery

Explore the city's cool area of Kelham Island, making sure to schedule in a pitstop at this oasis of speciality coffee, handcrafted pastries and springy sourdough. Take your flattie and bun to-go or grab a table in the roomy industrial-style cafe.

92 Burton Road, Sheffield, South Yorkshire, S3 8BX

thedepotbakery.co.uk ◎ thedepotbakery ⅋

47 Tamper Coffee Sellers Wheel

Visit for a delicious slice of Kiwi coffee 'n' brunch culture in a cool reinvented industrial building. Quality caffeination is assured, as is a sociable time in this buzzy spot where as much attention is paid to the brews as the delicious edibles.

149 Arundel Street, Sheffield, South Yorkshire, S1 2NU

tampercoffee.co.uk ◎ tampercoffeesw

Eve Kitchen

48 Eve Kitchen

Pillowy doughnuts in a rainbow of boutique flavours are paired with well-made speciality brews at this spot on Sheffield's bohemian Sharrow Vale Road. In summer, espresso is partnered with homemade soft-serve ice cream for next-level affogatos.

380 Sharrow Vale Road, Sheffield, South Yorkshire, S11 8ZP

49 Forge Bakehouse

Forge deals in the best things in life. Its own-roasted speciality coffee and top-notch carbs are handcrafted each day by the crew's baristas, bakers and roasters. This Abbeydale Road spot is sister to other sites in the city and two in Dronfield and Chesterfield.

302 Abbeydale Road, Sheffield, South Yorkshire, S7 1F

forgebakehouse.co.uk forgebakehouse

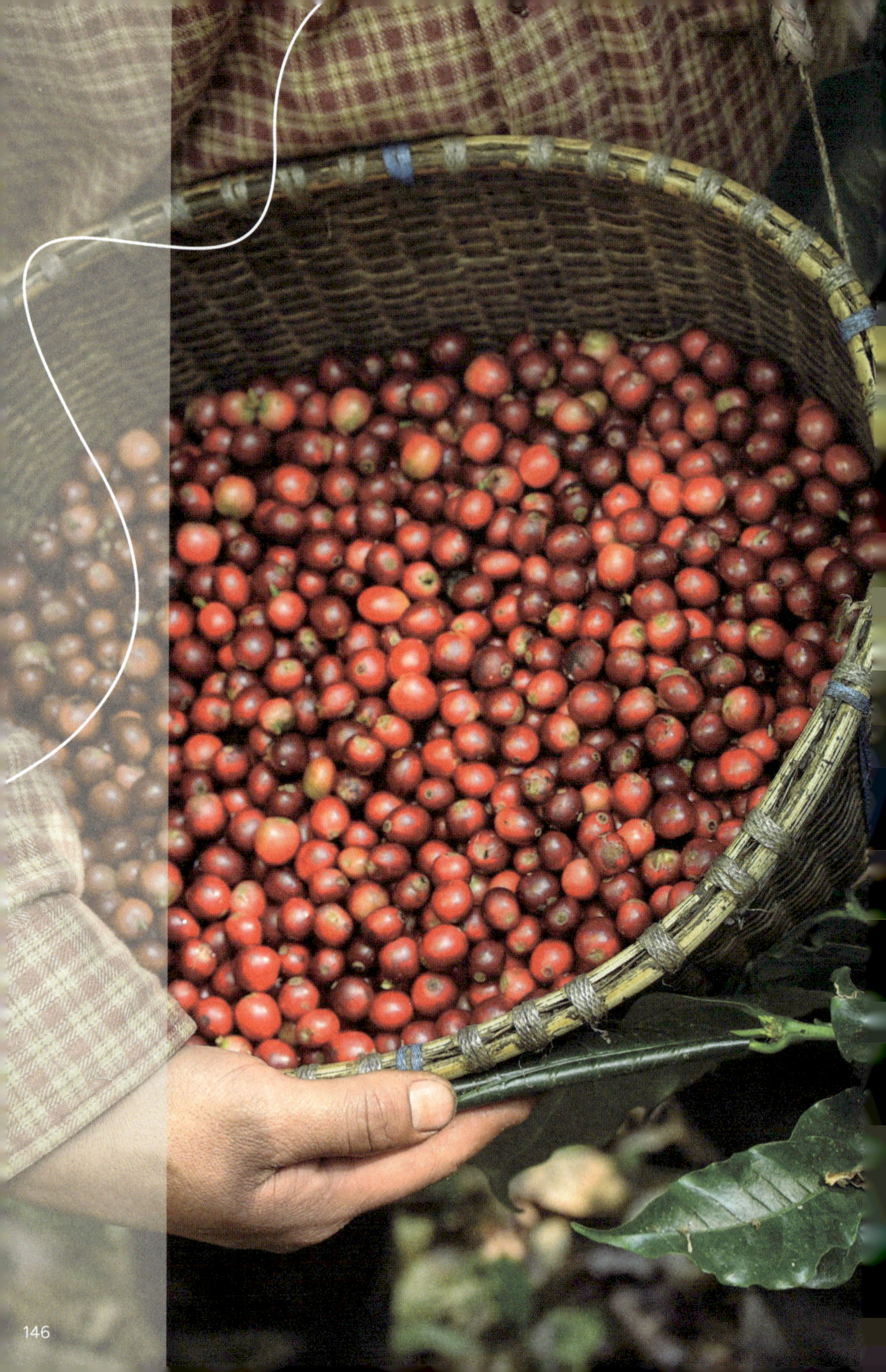

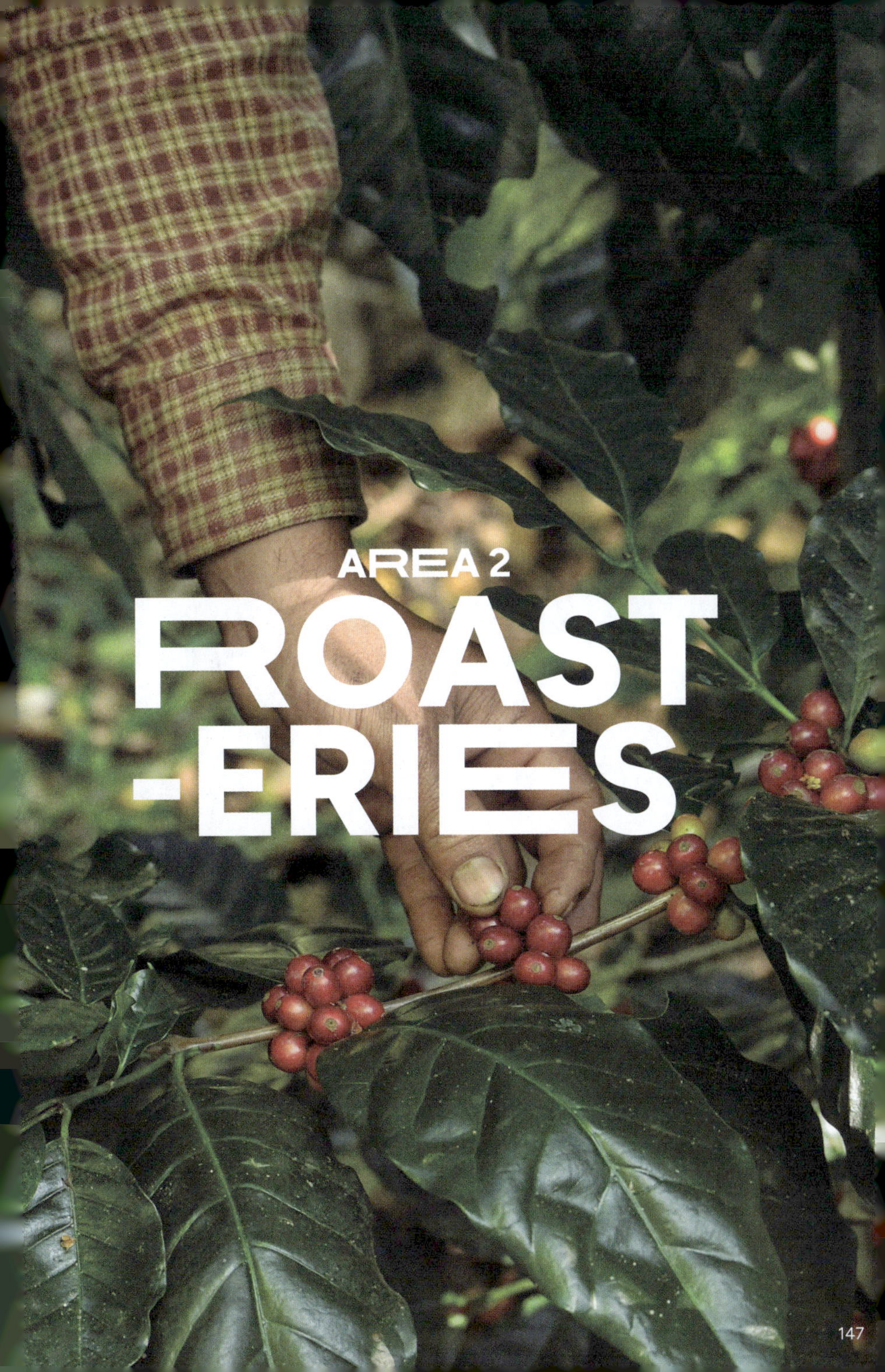

AREA 2 ROAST-ERIES

Pink Lane Coffee

50 Pink Lane Coffee

As a result of its sustainable sourcing, fair payment to farmers and use of single-origin beans only, this Newcastle roastery is guaranteed to leave customers feeling in the pink. Shop the beans online or swing by its cafe to pick up bags and to sample beans as perfect pours.

1 Pink Lane, Newcastle, NE1 5DW

pinklanecoffee.co.uk
🄾 pinklanecoffeecollective

51 Ouseburn Coffee Co.

This roastery has been keeping the North East well caffeinated since 2012. Its beans can be found at outlets across the region, including its own cafe, Harvest, in Jesmond and its concession at Fenwick Foodhall. On weekends grab a brew to-go at Tynemouth Station Market.

Albion Row, Ouseburn, Newcastle, NE6 1LQ

ouseburncoffee.co.uk 🄾 ouseburncoffee

Rounton Coffee Roasters

East Rounton, Northallerton, North Yorkshire, DL6 2LG

rountoncoffee.co.uk | 01609 765034

 rountoncoffeeroasters rountoncoffeeroasters

SIPPED THAT · SIPPED THAT · SIPPED THAT · SIPPED THAT

It's been just over a decade since Rounton fired up its first roaster, and the team recently celebrated in true coffee-fanatic style by installing their dream machine – a Loring S35 Kestrel.

Even before the swanky roaster arrived, Rounton was bagging awards quicker than you can say 'single origin'. Get a behind-the-scenes look at the roastery by taking a tour (make an appointment first). The team source beans from coffee farmers across the world, bringing different regional coffees and a rainbow of flavour profiles to their portfolio.

'Rounton has been bagging awards quicker than you can say 'single origin''

With environmental protection front of mind, Rounton became partners of 1% For The Planet, pledging to donate one per cent of its turnover to environmental charities. Close to its heart are local organisations Yorkshire Wildlife Trust, Ouseburn Trust and Ribble Rivers Trust. The roastery also supports the ACE 2030 – an initiative to improve farming infrastructure and plant trees in the Rwenzori Mountains in Uganda.

Rounton's philanthropic goals don't end there: through its commitment pledge, it has its sights set on working with more local environmental organisations in order to support the community.

Established
2014

Roaster make & size
Loring S35 Kestrel
35kg

Northallerton

Roost Coffee & Roastery

Unit 8 Malton Enterprise Park, 15 Cherry Farm Close, Malton,
North Yorkshire, YO17 6AR | roostcoffee.co.uk | 01653 697635

 roostcoffeeandroastery roostcoffee

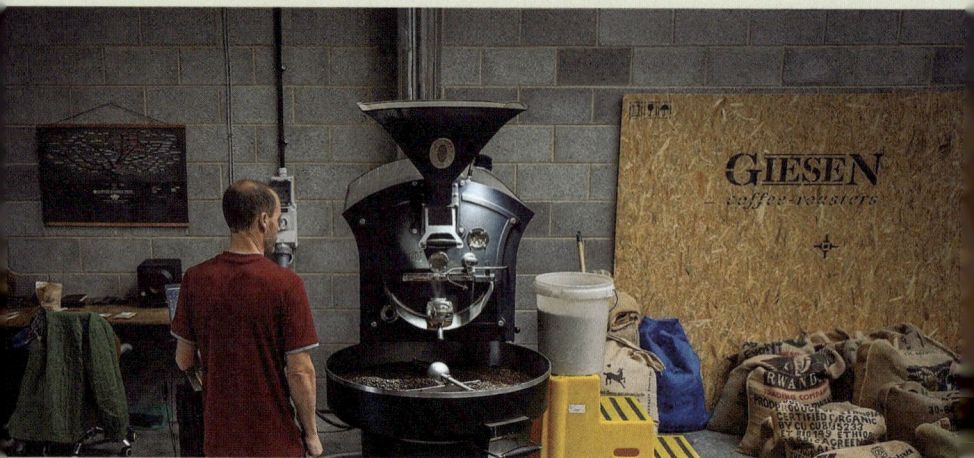

Housed in a spanking new roastery with fully electric roasting powered by renewable energy, this family-run business is proud to have reduced its emissions by a whopping 90 per cent by switching from its gas roaster. This, along with the sleek rebranded packaging, has breathed new life into the ten-year-old roastery. Creating quality speciality coffee at an affordable price remains the main priority, a focus that's been woven into the fabric of Roost since the get-go by owners Ruth and David Elkington.

'The family-run business has reduced its emissions by a whopping 90 per cent'

The team continue to supply a wide selection of blends and single origins to customers through both the website and Roost's espresso bar and retail shop in Talbot Yard. Avid coffee fans will want to check out the Roost Coffee Club to receive a handpicked selection of beans each month, which arrive whole or ground to their specifications.

The coffee is sourced through trusted importers and, at any one time, the collection includes at least one filter blend, two espresso blends, two chemical-free Swiss Water decafs and 12 single origins from across the globe.

Established
2015

Roaster make & size
Giesen W15E 15kg,
Giesen W6E 6kg

Malton

The Clubhouse Roasters

18 Newmarket Street, Skipton, North Yorkshire, BD23 2HR

theclubhousecc.co.uk | 07808 831523

 theclubhousecc theclubhouseroasters

Clubhouse claims the title of the 'only nano roaster in the Yorkshire Dales', and cooks up a small-but-perfectly-formed menu of single-origin beans from across the globe. The unstoppable force behind the pint-size operation is Kane Pulford-Roberts, whose passion for beans and brews led to him opening the roastery in 2019.

Community is the name of the game at Clubhouse and its spin-offs include a running club, after-dark evenings with cocktails and nibbles, and events such as wine tastings.

'Clubhouse claims the title of the "only nano roaster in the Yorkshire Dales"'

However, high-grade coffee remains at the heart of the operation. Kane's trips to origin have enabled him to develop direct relationships with farmers such as Roger Chilcon, owner of three hectares of coffee plants in the El Diamante village of San Jose de Lourdes in Peru. Roger grows yellow and red caturra at 1,900m altitude. His cherries are picked as ripe as possible before being pre-fermented overnight in bags. The macerated fruit is then depulped and fermented for 24–36 hours: the extended fermentation and cherry maceration gives the cup a pronounced fruity note which complements the citric acidity that results from high altitude.

Kane has primarily served his roasts at the on-site cafe, but Clubhouse's popularity has been such that he's going wholesale. Find his coffees in local cafes and Michelin-starred restaurant The Angel at Hetton.

Established
2019

Roaster make & size
BlueKing 2kg

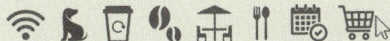

Skipton

55 North Star Coffee Roasters

Unit 32 The Boulevard, Leeds Dock, Leeds, West Yorkshire, LS10 1PZ

northstarroast.com | 01138 244230

northstarcoffeeroasters   northstarroast

Alex and Holly Kragiopoulos, founders of North Star, began their relationship with coffee in 2011 while conducting research in Kenya for their dissertation. The trip had a profound impact on them, highlighting both the beauty of coffee production and the complexities and injustices of its supply chain.

They returned home determined to make a positive impact in the industry, an ambition that resulted in the establishment of North Star Coffee Roasters in 2013. The roastery became the first of its kind in Leeds and continues to shape Yorkshire's thriving speciality coffee scene.

'Visitors can immerse themselves in all things coffee at the new North Star Coffee Hub'

Every North Star bean sold contributes directly to the team's efforts at source. So far they've established and funded two pioneering projects in El Salvador and Rwanda, building resilience in the supply chain.

Visitors can immerse themselves in all things coffee at the new North Star Coffee Hub, which offers various training courses, before visiting the roastery's Leeds Dock coffee shop next door to sample the full gamut of beans and enjoy a delicious seasonal brunch.

A takeout fix can also be found at the North Star Kiosk on Sovereign Street, which sells the full range of coffee beans, alongside rotating espresso options and seasonal batch brews.

Established
2013

Roaster make & size
Loring S35,
Loring S15

Leeds

152

Limini Coffee

Unit 6 Luddite Way Business Park, Rawfolds Way, Cleckheaton,
West Yorkshire, BD19 5DQ | liminicoffee.co.uk | 01274 911419

liminicoffee

Fuelled by espresso and driven by customer happiness, the Limini squad has, for 15 years, roasted and supplied speciality-grade coffee across the country.

To delve deeper into the cherry-to-cup process and better understand life at origin, the team of caficionados recently took a trip to Brazil to visit Fazenda Pinhal and farmer Pedro Gabarra, with whom they enjoy a close partnership.

And, if further proof of their dedication to crafting exceptional coffee was needed, they also recently invested in a lauded ACS Vostok Lever. The state-of-the-art espresso machine makes it easier for the team to extract the nuanced flavour profiles from each roast.

'To delve deeper into the cherry-to-cup process, the team recently visited farmer Pedro Gabarra in Brazil'

Precious greens sourced from Brazil, alongside finds from El Salvador and India, are carefully bronzed into espresso blends Limini, Limini Dark Roast, Liscio, Kata, Rimini and Blue Mountain. Countries including Costa Rica, Ethiopia, Guatemala, Rwanda and Colombia form the backbone of the single-origin roasts. A whole range of decafs and limited-edition releases also feature.

Established
2008

Roaster make & size
Loring S35 Kestral
35kg x 2

Cleckheaton

White Rose Coffee Roasters

6-8 Hall Street, Halifax, West Yorkshire, HX1 5AY

whiterosecoffeeroasters.co.uk | 01422 347734

whiteroseroasters white.rose.coffee.roasters

There's no shortage of choice for coffee lovers browsing the online shop of this independent Halifax roastery. With over 22 single origins and eight bespoke blends (including three Great Taste award winners) available at any time, it's a treasure trove for those who enjoy sampling coffees from different regions.

From Burundi to Colombia, Jamaica to Papua New Guinea, founder Robert Cooper scours the world for beans of quality and provenance. He favours supporting small plantations and sourcing beans that have undergone anaerobic fermentation, are honey processed, or are exclusive varietals such as geisha. These precious greens are bronzed on a duo of Toper roasters', by a team with over 30 years' experience in the industry, before being packaged in fully recyclable bags.

'A treasure trove for those who enjoy sampling coffees from different regions'

Those who eschew experimentation in favour of the comfort of familiarity will find it in White Rose's selection of blends: Cattle Market Espresso and Hikers Inspiration are the most popular and can be bought as whole bean or pre-ground. Ambitious coffee fans can even buy green beans to roast at home.

Coffee shops and restaurants looking to craft their own bespoke roast can take advantage of White Rose's white label service.

Established
2015

Roaster make & size
Toper 30kg,
Toper 5kg

Halifax

Dark Woods Coffee

Holme Mills, West Slaithwaite Road, Marsden, West Yorkshire, HD7 6LS

darkwoodscoffee.co.uk | 01484 843141

 darkwoodscoffee darkwoodscoffee

This roastery, barista school and pop-up cafe may be housed in a Victorian textile mill and the building set amid ancient woodland, but Dark Woods is an adventurous coffee pioneer utilising contemporary roasting methods.

Its blend of tradition and innovation has won the roastery multiple awards, including over 100 Great Taste awards – and three of its Golden Forks. Not that this success should come as any surprise given that the roastery's trio of directors (Damian Blackburn, Paul Meikle-Janney and Ian Agnew) have, between them, judged the Cup of Excellence, helped organise the World Coffee Championships, co-written the SCA barista qualifications and chaired Farmers' Voice Radio (a charity that uses local radio stations to assist coffee farmers around the world).

'Dark Woods has won multiple awards, including over 100 Great Taste awards'

The team's experience and expertise have resulted in relationships with top-notch bean producers and distributors who are keen to share their best beans with the roastery, confident they'll be in good hands. The output of these relationships is Dark Woods' Producer Series which showcases exclusive seasonal micro-lots and runs alongside its Core Range of winning blends and single origins.

Visit the website to find out when the roastery is open for pop-up events, and to stock up on beans via the click and collect service.

Established
2013

Roaster make & size
Probat G45 45kg,
Probat UG22 22kg,
Probat 5 5kg

Marsden

Danelaw Coffee

Unit D11, Gate 4, Meltham Mills Industrial Estate, Meltham, Holmfirth, West Yorkshire, HD9 4DS | danelaw.coffee | 07506 900331

danelawcoffee danelawcoffee

Founded in April 2022 by two-time Coffee in Good Spirits champion David Jameson, this Yorkshire roastery takes its moniker from the Viking name for the north and east of England. Located in a former tractor factory, it has quickly built a reputation as a quality-coffee hotspot.

David has 20 years' experience in the coffee industry which he uses to make speciality accessible to all. Coffee-curious consumers will find the online shop uses clear language and relatable flavour references, while coffee businesses enjoy a range of support, training and equipment.

'Decaf drinkers deserve great coffee too'

Several coffees in Danelaw's catalogue of blends and single origins have won Great Taste awards, including the lightly roasted Fjødr, and Mjolká – a darker blend that remains 100 per cent speciality arabica.

The team are (quite rightly) adamant that decaf drinkers deserve great coffee too, so have developed four house decafs. These include Nott Fjødr, which won a three-star award at the 2024 Great Taste awards. Regularly changing guest decafs also feature.

A newly opened coffee shop in Holmfirth is the place to sample the roastery's espresso blends, decaffeinated coffees from the Nott Coffee range and single origins from producers the team have visited and worked with for years.

Established
2022

Roaster make & size
Giesen W6E 6kg,
Aillio Bullet 1kg

Holmfirth

Yellow Bear Roasters

Yellow Bear, Hollowgate, Holmfirth, West Yorkshire, HD9 2DG

bearbeans.co.uk | 07304 048342

bearbeans_

The high-calibre coffee bronzed by the Yellow Bear team has been lauded since founder Chris Gregory established the roastery in 2019.

Its recent first-place victory at the Mercanta International Roasting competition – where Yellow Bear triumphed over 24 of Europe's finest roasteries – shone a spotlight on its impeccable beans and respected status. The win reaffirmed what loyal customers have long known: while Chris and team take a refreshingly inclusive approach to speciality coffee, without a whisper of elitism, they are serious about the art of roasting.

'A recent first-place victory shone a spotlight on its impeccable beans and respected status'

The team produce a diverse portfolio of single origins and blends, all ethically and responsibly sourced. The range includes classic washed profiles, expertly crafted naturals, experimental fermentations and fruity co-ferments.

Kickstart the Yellow Bear flavour odyssey with Bear Necessities (a versatile everyday espresso blend), Brown Bear (a redefined dark roast), and new experimental filter blend Red Panda (funky, exotic and adventurous).

Discover more cracking coffees by visiting the Coffee House roastery outlet in Holmfirth. Here you'll find at least eight coffees available to sample, complemented by freshly baked pastries from local artisans.

Established
2019

Roaster make & size
Golden 5kg

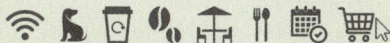

Holmfirth

61 Forge Coffee Roasters

Don Road, Sheffield, South Yorkshire, S9 2TF

forgecoffeeroasters.co.uk | 01142 441361

 forgeroasters forgeroasters

A homage to Sheffield's proud industrial heritage lies at the heart of this city roastery, which includes some sartorial nods to the past. Not only do the team sport baker-boy caps and meticulously trimmed moustaches, but they also drive a vintage delivery truck and own a fascinating collection of forging memorabilia.

The Giesen W30 that roasts the beans may be contemporary and efficient but it also oozes charm as it churns out small batches of exquisite speciality-grade coffee.

'A homage to Sheffield's proud industrial heritage'

The team craft four blends, one of which is a decaf. The perennially popular crowd-pleaser is Invicta, a delicious espresso brimming with notes of black cherry, dark chocolate, toffee and vanilla. For big-eyed bean fans there's also a changing line-up of handpicked, washed and fermented single-origin coffees to explore.

Inspired by the craftsmanship and creativity of the 'city of steel', the team are committed to offering expertise to the coffee industry. They are long-term suppliers of La Marzocco machines and offer service, support and training. They also supply the handmade-in-Florence Eureka range so home brewers can get in on the action.

Established
2015

Roaster make & size
Giesen W30 30kg,
Giesen W1A 1kg,
IKAWA

Sheffield

158

62 Cuppers Choice

Take a tour of the world's coffee regions, varietals and processing methods without leaving South Yorkshire. Sheffield's proudly independent roastery cooks up everything on a clean Loring S15 Falcon. Beans are sold wholesale to cafes, and online in small bags to home brewers.

Unit F1, G4, 19-21 Carlisle Street, Sheffield, South Yorkshire, S4 7QN

cupperschoice.coffee 🅾 cupperschoice

Limini Coffee

Unit 6 Luddite Way Business Park, Rawfolds Way, Cleckheaton,
West Yorkshire, BD19 5DQ | liminicoffee.co.uk | 01274 911419

liminicoffee

COFFEE TRAINER

Since 2008, Limini's How To Start A Coffee Shop course has turned many novices into successful coffee shop owners.

'The feedback from our students is that the training is very beneficial — and we see this when we visit their shops,' says founder Youri Vlag.

The popular course is held at Limini's dedicated training facility and roastery in Yorkshire and it teaches participants on a variety of equipment types and barista brewing tools, as well as a roaster. The practical syllabus covers all aspects of starting and running a coffee shop, and offers plenty of ongoing support and advice on completion.

'It's very hands-on with close supervision by the barista trainer'

'We built the centre for the sole purpose of barista training,' adds Youri. *'It's designed so each student has a workstation to themselves and feels relaxed. It's very hands-on with close supervision by the barista trainer.'*

As a speciality coffee supplier and roastery, Limini prides itself on a friendly, professional service and the team offer a plethora of experience in serving, roasting and training in all things coffee.

Established
2008

Cleckheaton

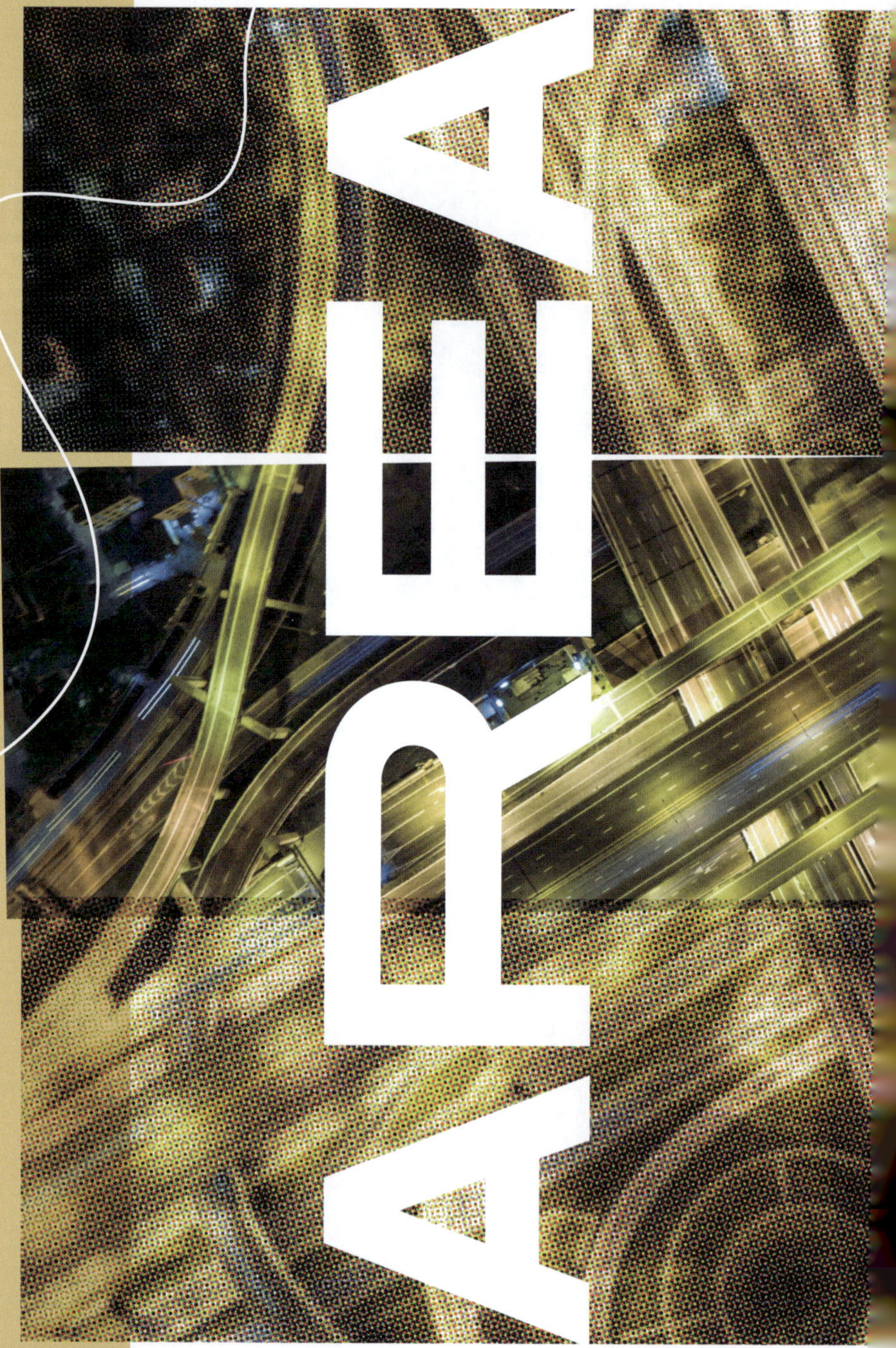
AREA

Area 3

● Coffee shops

1 Ginger and Co.
2 Nexus Cafe
3 The Birds Nest
4 Guilt Trip
5 JNCTN
6 Bayleys
7 Saint Kitchen
8 Faculty Coffee
9 Wayland's Yard
10 Perch
11 Bean & Leaf Coffee House
12 Fueled Speciality Coffee
13 Been Coffee
14 St Martin's
   Coffee Shop & Kitchen
15 Saints of Mokha
16 København Espresso Bar
17 The Coffee Obsessive
18 The Wandering Goblin
19 Cartwheel
20 Punch Coffee
21 Effy
22 Dispatch
23 Cosmos
24 Lions Cafe
25 Circus Head
26 Fika Norwich
27 The Yard Coffee
28 The Lawn Cafe
29 Shou Coffee
30 Flock

Locations are approximate

Peak District
National Park

23
22
21
20
19
37 18
DERBY
NOTTINGHAM

Eccleshall
33

12

13

Shrewsbury
3
1

Shropshire Hills
National Landscape

Cannock
Chase National
Landscape
10
9
8
32 7
BIRMINGHAM
2

LEICESTER 14
15
16
17

COVENTRY
11

31

Kidderminster

Bromsgrove
6

Royal Leamington Spa

5
WORCESTER
4

Northampton

HEREFORD Malvern Hills
National
Landscape

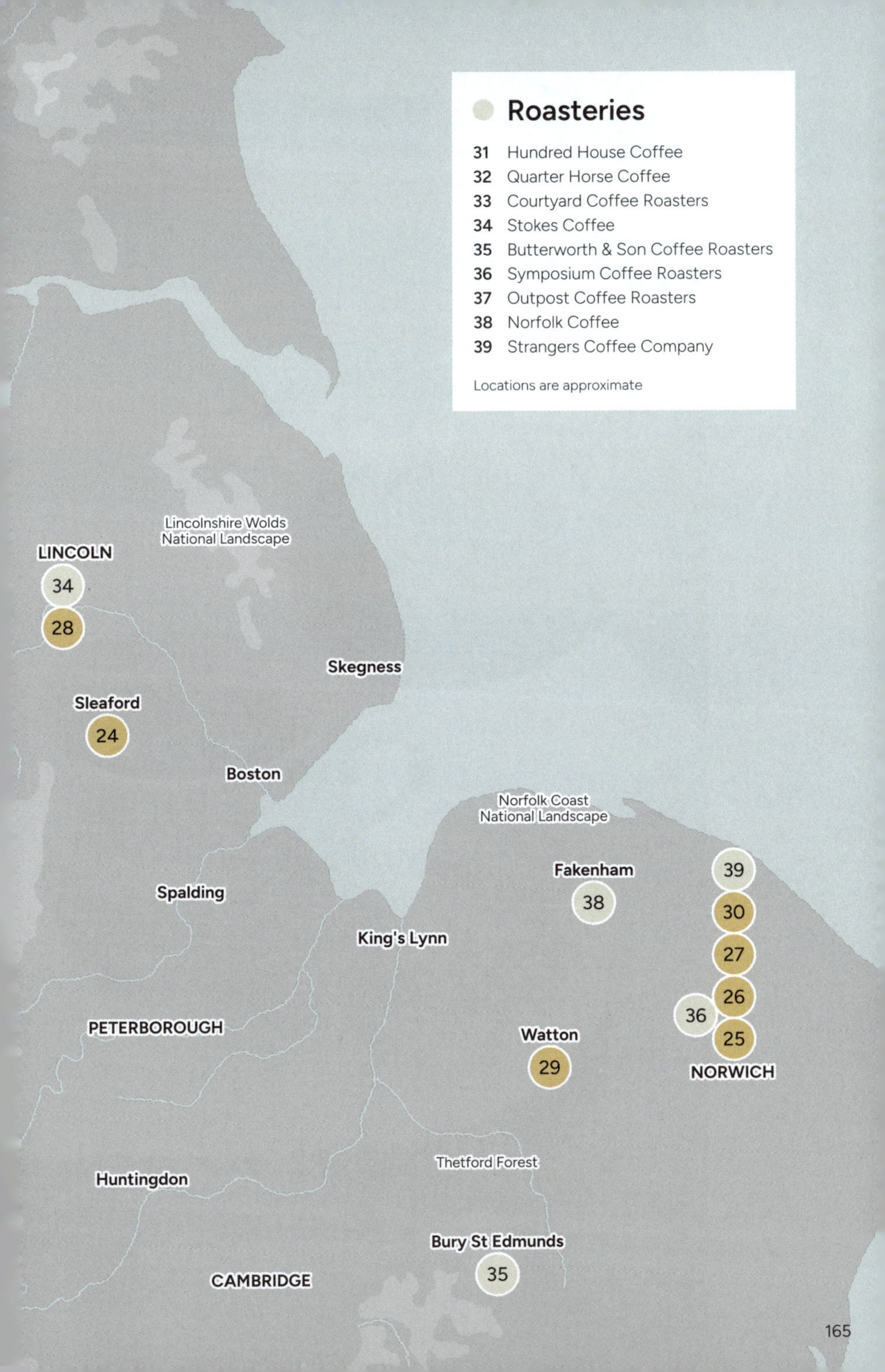

Roasteries

31 Hundred House Coffee
32 Quarter Horse Coffee
33 Courtyard Coffee Roasters
34 Stokes Coffee
35 Butterworth & Son Coffee Roasters
36 Symposium Coffee Roasters
37 Outpost Coffee Roasters
38 Norfolk Coffee
39 Strangers Coffee Company

Locations are approximate

Lincolnshire Wolds
National Landscape

LINCOLN
34
28

Skegness

Sleaford
24

Boston

Norfolk Coast
National Landscape

Spalding

Fakenham
38

King's Lynn

39
30
27
26
36
25
NORWICH

PETERBOROUGH

Watton
29

Huntingdon

Thetford Forest

Bury St Edmunds
35

CAMBRIDGE

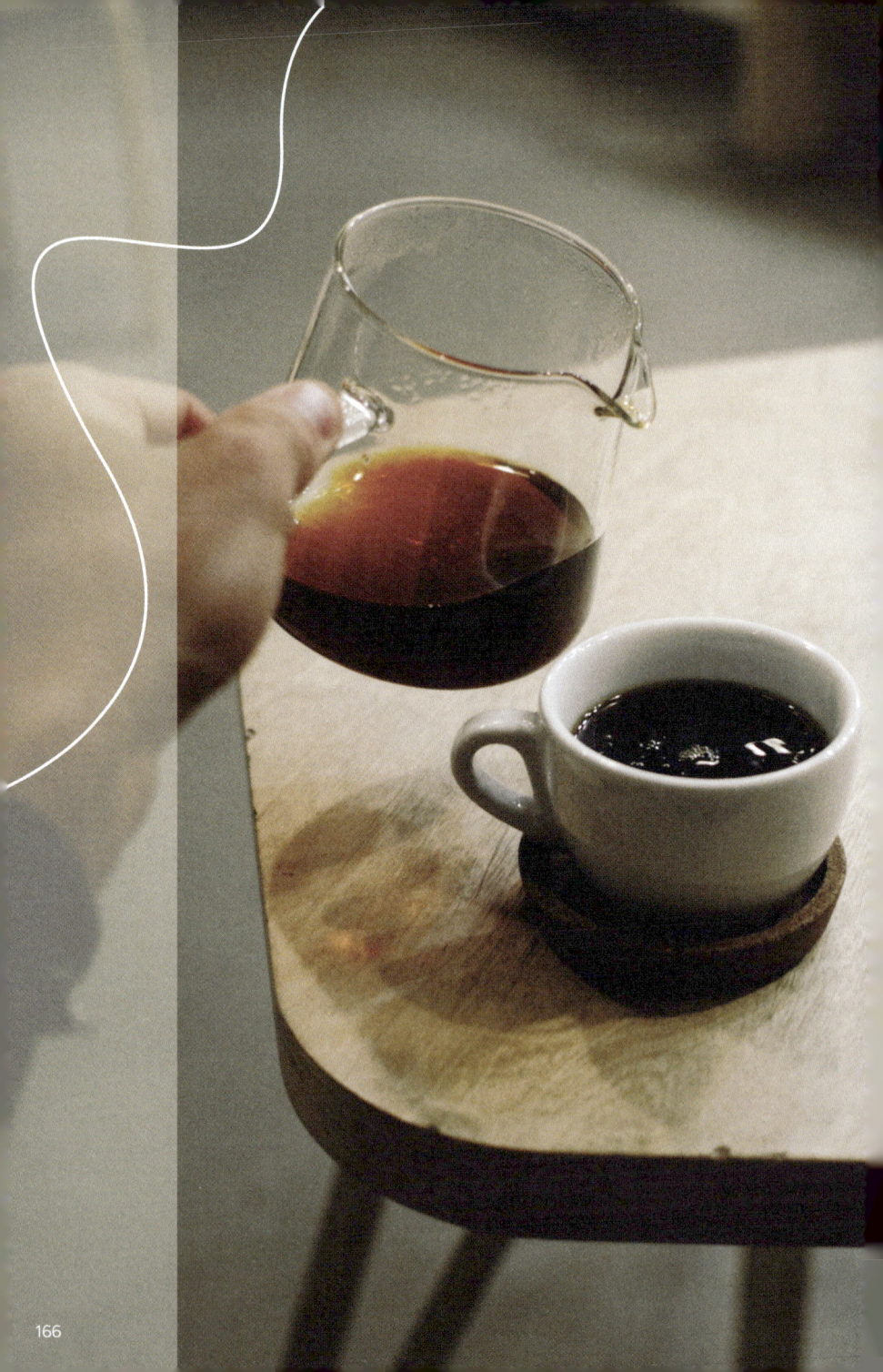

AREA 3

COFFEE SHOPS

① Ginger & Co.

30-31 Princess Street, Shrewsbury, Shropshire, SY1 1LW
gingerandcocoffeeshop.co.uk | 07830 704090

 gingerandcocoffee ginger_and_co_coffee

Ginger & Co. owner and experienced barista Melody Facchin has the speciality cafe experience nailed.

The coffee – a bespoke blend supplied by Method Coffee Roasters – is consistently delicious, crafted by Melody and her pro team who know exactly how to eke out the nuanced flavours from every dose. Single-origin guest options tend to spotlight Ethiopian, Mexican and Colombian beans and are fashioned into V60 and pourover drinks which sparkle in clarity.

🐾 Pups are very welcome – there's even a dedicated dog wall

Another non-negotiable ingredient in creating a stonking cafe experience is seasonal homemade food, which the Ginger & Co. crew craft with aplomb. Everything – from the pukka porridge, soups and toasties to the luscious cakes and bejewelled traybakes – is made in-house and from scratch using local produce. There's always an impressive assortment of veggie, vegan and gluten-free options too (the vegan carrot cake is a perennial fave).

The cherry on top is a cosy space that's complemented by warm service. It's a lovely environment in which to slow down and take pleasure in every sip of handcrafted coffee and bite of homemade cake.

Established
2015

Key roastery
Method Coffee Roasters

Brewing method
Espresso, V60, pourover

Machine
La Marzocco Linea AV

Grinder
Mahlkonig K30, Mahlkonig EK43

Opening hours
Mon-Thu
8.30am-3pm
Fri-Sat
8.30am-4pm
Sun
10am-3pm

Shrewsbury

168

(2) Nexus Cafe

38 Meriden Street, Birmingham, West Midlands, B5 5LS

nexuscafe.co.uk | 07742 149976

Nexus cafe nexus.cafe_

Venturing into Nexus – a fresh face on the Brum coffee scene – is a little like stepping into nature: upon entering, guests encounter a lush plant wall lined with mirrors, as well as warm lighting and accents in wood. It's a wonderfully inviting environment in which the team cultivate an accessible and welcoming hub that draws in creatives, speciality coffee geeks and casual coffee sippers.

Birmingham buddies New Era supply the house beans for espresso, while the caffeine curious are delighted by a whirligig of guest roasts for pourovers. The likes of Blossom, Atkinsons, KillBean and Lucid provide fresh flavours to sample on a monthly basis.

Check out the funky coffee cups, which mimic disposable plastic cups but are ceramic

One of Nexus' specialisms is the pourover and the team serve coffee via V60, Origami, Chemex, Kalita and OREA kit. Batch brew is also on the agenda to appear in the near future. Pair your speciality brew with a bagel or toastie (they're made fresh each day in-house).

Coffee's not the only enticing thing about the Nexus experience; the team also hold events, including live jazz, poetry nights and art classes.

Established
2024

Key roastery
New Era
Coffee Roasters

Brewing method
Filter, V60, Chemex,
Kalita Wave, Orea,
Origami Dripper

Machine
Victoria Arduino
Eagle One

Grinder
Mythos,
Mahlkonig EK43,
Eukera Zenith 65,
zeroHero z5 Manual
Coffee Grinder,
Comandante C40

Opening hours
Mon-Fri
9am-6pm
Sat-Sun
10am-6pm

Birmingham

169

JNCTN

3 The Birds Nest

Set amid the vibrant and eclectic stalls of indie-rich Shrewsbury Market Hall, The Birds Nest is a lively spot for animated chat, carefully prepped espresso and classic street-food dishes. Savour flavours from across the globe in crowd-pleasers such as thai pork meatballs and tofu bhaji burger.

The Market Hall, Claremont Street, Shrewsbury, Shropshire, SY1 1HQ

thebirdsnestcafe.co.uk ⓞ thebirdsnestcafe

5 JNCTN

Fully traceable, sustainably sourced and freshly roasted coffee is reason enough to seek out this slick Worcester hangout. However, it's also a great shout for a banging brunch, teas from eteaket and freshly whizzed smoothies. In a rush? The counter is replenished daily with seductive sarnies, salads, pastries and cakes to-go.

14 Foregate Street, Worcester, WR1 1DB

jnctn-worcester.co.uk ⓞ jnctn.worcester

4 Guilt Trip

Ain't nothing to feel guilty about here. In all three of its locations (find them in Broadway and Cheltenham, too) Guilt Trip serves quality coffee alongside dairy from local producers and carbs crafted in their own bakery. Sink into caffeine submission while hoovering up one of the 12 doughnut flavours. Salted Caramel Twix, anyone?

Unit B Matthew House, Weir Lane, Worcester, WR2 4AY

guilttripcoffeeanddonuts.co.uk
ⓞ guilttrip_uk

6 Bayleys

A high-energy vibe, pumping music and craft beer are just three of the reasons Bayleys is so loved by locals. During the day though, it's the coffee and cake that bring the joy. The crew may be serious about caffeine but its served without pretention, so feel free to dunk that donut.

6 Worcester Road, Bromsgrove, B61 7AE

ⓞ bayleys_of_bromsgrove

Wayland's Yard

7 Saint Kitchen

Banging bagels stuffed with fillings like lamb merguez, tzatziki and chilli sauce sit on the menu next to puffy pancakes, sourdough toasties and cinnamon buns at this Jewellery Quarter cafe. Pair your picks of the menu with quality brews. Check out its two sister cafes in Warwickshire.

St Paul's Square, Birmingham, B3 1QS

saintkitchen.com 🅾 saintkitchen

8 Faculty Coffee

Hidden away in historic Piccadilly Arcade in the heart of the city, this is a find for top-notch speciality caffeine and homemade carbs like pastel de nata and buns. The well-crafted brews and bakes are served with friendly vibes. Don't leave without checking out the retail selection of beans to-go and coffee kit.

14 Piccadilly Arcade, Birmingham, B2 4HD

facultycoffee.com 🅾 faculty.coffee

10 Perch

Hunt out this sleek cafe for next-level pastries, cakes, brunches and well-crafted coffee. As you queue for a table, the glass counter stuffed with exquisite viennoiserie is super seductive, but don't make your pick until you've perused the brunch menu of goodies like turkish eggs and delicious toppings on toast.

St John Cadbury House, 190 Corporation Street, Birmingham, B4 6QD

perchbakery.co.uk 🅾 perch.bakery

9 Wayland's Yard

This speciality coffee fave is a large and buzzy place to catch up with chums and work through a funky menu of banging brunches and well-prepped brews. Find a sister outlet in Worcester and look out for a new baby of the bunch which will be launched in 2025.

42 Bull St, Birmingham, B4 6AF

waylandsyard.co.uk 🅾 waylandsyard

11 Bean & Leaf Coffee House

Warm and fuzzy vibes rule at this family-run spot, where perfectly-prepped brews are crafted from house- and guest-roasted beans and served alongside homemade toasties, cakes and pastries. There's plenty for tea drinkers too – a timer comes with each infusion to guarantee the perfect pour.

75 Hertford Street, Coventry, CV1 1LB

beanandleafcoffeehouse.co.uk
🅾 beanandleafcoffeehouse

Fueled Speciality Coffee

4 Carters Square, Uttoxeter, Staffordshire, ST14 7FN

fueledcoffee.co.uk

 fueledcoffeeuk fueledcoffeeuk

In 2017, Joe Ingleton retired from professional dancing with the dream of making his next adventure the launch of his own coffee shop. To learn the tricks of the trade, he enrolled at the London School of Coffee. Then, in 2021, Joe opened the doors of Fueled in Uttoxeter.

The bright and spacious cafe introduced a cosmopolitan vibe to the market town and has become known for its fun-loving staff, belt-busting brunches and quality coffee.

Buxton Coffee Roasters supplies the house blend, a fusion of Brazilian, Ethiopian and Thai beans that reveals notes of chocolate and hazelnut with a citrusy zing. Customers can keep visits fresh by sampling the rotating selection of single-origin guest roasts.

🔵 Download the digital loyalty card to claim your free hot drink

Leading the food line-up is The Auckland, a bagel stuffed with pesto, avocado, streaky bacon, cream cheese and balsamic glaze. Inspired by Joe's travels in New Zealand, it's become a customer fave. Fans of the trad full English should order The Fully Fueled which includes hash browns and crisp black pudding.

Drawing on Joe's roots in the entertainment industry, the team also host regular events, including comedy gigs, creative workshops and mediumship nights.

Established
2021

Key roastery
Buxton Coffee Roasters

Brewing method
Espresso, V60, Chemex, Curtis Seraphim

Machine
Sanremo Opera

Grinder
Mahlkonig E65S, Mahlkonig E65S GbW, Mahlkonig EK43, Mahlkonig E80

Opening hours
Mon-Thu
7.30am-5pm
Fri-Sat
7.30am-6pm
Sun
9am-4pm

Uttoxeter

13 Been Coffee

Derby and Burton Services, Willington, Derbyshire, DE65 6DX

been.coffee | 07592 294650

 beencoffeeuk beencoffeeuk

A service station with an independent cafe is a rare sight, but one that serves speciality-grade coffee and freshly made food? It's almost too good to be true. No wonder discerning coffee drinkers often plan pit stops – or even reroute their journeys – just to enjoy a quality cup at Been Coffee.

Located at Derby and Burton Services on the outskirts of Derby, this is a hidden gem where travellers of the A38 and A50 can refuel with creamy oat lattes and delicious road-trip fare.

Speciality beans come courtesy of London roastery Ozone and are crafted into first-rate espresso drinks via a Nuova Simonelli machine. The cafe also features a wildcard guest roast from Crown & Canvas in Staffordshire, while Nottingham's Outpost Coffee provides a fruitier option on filter. Hot drinks extend to a range of loose-leaf teas and luxe hot chocolates.

Brews are best polished off with one of the house special bagels: the smoked salmon and philly cheese or New York-style pastrami are fan favourites. Alternatively, choose from an ever-changing seasonal menu.

🔸 It's not summer until Been's signature cold brew is on the menu – if you spy it, try it

Need to get back on the road in a hurry? Grab a bacon, sausage and egg cob with a cortado to-go. The team are environmentally conscious and use compostable packaging, avoid plastic, and prepare food from scratch on-demand – super rare at service stations.

Established
2021

Key roastery
Ozone Coffee Roasters

Brewing method
Espresso, filter

Machine
Nuova Simonelli Appia Life XT

Grinder
Markibar IZAGA

Opening hours
Mon-Fri
7am-5.30pm
Sat-Sun
7.30am-5.30pm

Willington

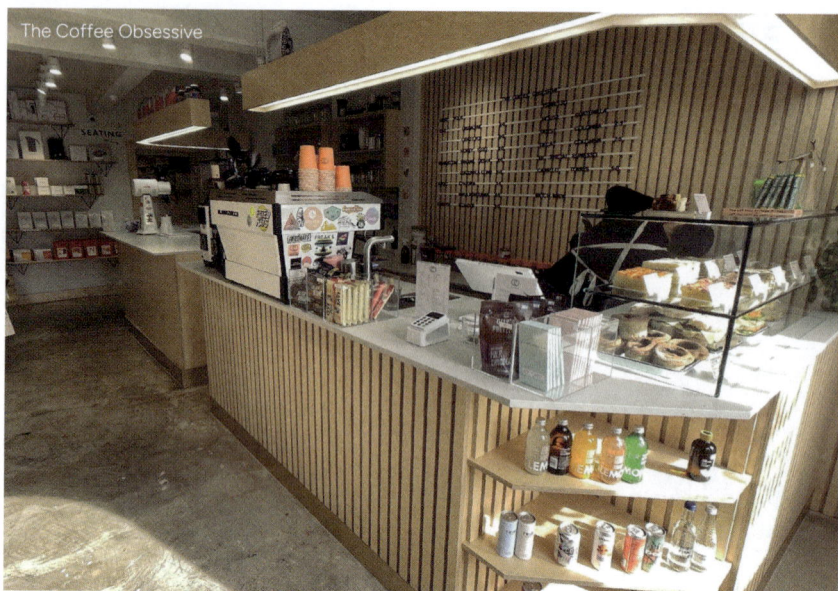
The Coffee Obsessive

14 St Martin's Coffee Shop & Kitchen

Take time out from a busy day and escape to this roomy cafe in Leicester's indie quarter. St Martin's is blessed with speciality brews and beautifully crafted homemade food in equal measure, so it's a no-brainer for a banging brunch.

2-6 St Martin's Walk, St Martin's Square, Leicester, LE1 5DG

stmartinscoffeeshop.co.uk
stmartinscoffeeshop

16 Køben Espresso Bar

Slick Scandi styling, quality brews and a lush corner-building setting attract coffee lovers from across the city and beyond. In winter, soak up the warmth of the sun through the beautiful rounded windows. In summer, grab an outside table and watch the world go by as you sip a flattie.

19 King St, Leicester, LE1 6RN
kobenespressobar

15 Saints of Mokha

It's worth making a pilgrimage to this Midlands roastery's airy city-centre coffee shop to sample its range of own-roasted beans and homemade food, as well as for pop-up music events and film screenings.

51-53 Belvoir Street, Leicester, LE1 6SL

saintsofmokha.com saintsofmokha

17 The Coffee Obsessive

This cafe's stripped-back contemporary style is influenced by founder Iqbal Mahomed's previous career in fashion, and matched by haute-couture-level beans. Each season's collection from international roasteries is handcrafted into beautifully styled caffeinated drinks.

53 Francis Street, Leicester, LE2 2BE

thecoffeeobsessive.com
thecoffeeobsessive

18 The Wandering Goblin

166 Derby Road, Nottingham, Nottinghamshire, NG7 1LR

thewanderinggoblin.com

wanderinggoblincoffee

When asked his inspiration for creating Wandering Goblin, owner Saul Aaron usually responds with: *'out of spite'*. But let's rephrase that: it was a response to coffee shops with poor working conditions, zero atmosphere and a sub-par offering, focusing on profit over pleasure.

At TWG, quality with transparency is the aim of the game and every aspect is subject to a great deal of care and attention – whether that's fair pay for staff or the quality of each item on the menu.

Pastries are sourdough-based and vegan: think houjicha and cocoa laminated pastry with chocolate filling

The menu may be niche – it serves just coffee, tea and pastries – yet the sheer range of those items is astonishing. The exclusive house roast from Cartwheel changes seasonally and is backed by a mammoth guest coffee board of between 8 and 14 coffees, all in stock and dialled in at any time. Recent showings have included beans from Coborn, Paso Paso, Cult, Radical Roasters, Nowhere Future Coffee Roasters, Formative and Killbean. The list changes every three to five weeks (usually swapping out 50 per cent at a time) so the array of styles, origins and roasteries offer something fresh to experience on every return visit.

There's also a major focus on tea, with every brew as carefully crafted as the coffees. Real matcha usucha and a range of traditional Japanese teas are served as multiple steeps.

Established
2023

Key roastery
Cartwheel Coffee Roasters

Brewing method
Espresso, Moccamaster, Origami Dripper

Machine
ACS Vostok

Grinder
Mahlkonig EK43

Opening hours
Mon-Fri
7.30am-5pm
Sat
8.30am-4pm
Sun
9am-4pm

Nottingham

19 Cartwheel

Swing by to sample own-roasted coffees
bronzed at Cartwheel's Sneinton HQ. Seasonal
brunch and lunch dishes plus lush buns and
pastries complement the speciality slurps,
high-grade teas and hot choc. Nab a cosy spot
indoors or sip outdoors on the partially covered
heated terrace.

1 Stoney Street, Beeston, Nottingham, NG9 2LA

cartwheelcoffee.com ◯ cartwheelcoffee

20 Punch Coffee

The warm vibe and good food and coffee
served at this friendly cafe have turned it into
a community hub. Join the locals who flock
to Punch for the knockout brews and bakes,
toasties and breakfast dishes which are crafted
from scratch each day.

215 Mansfield Road, Nottingham, NG1 3FS

punch.coffee ◯ punchcoffeenottingham

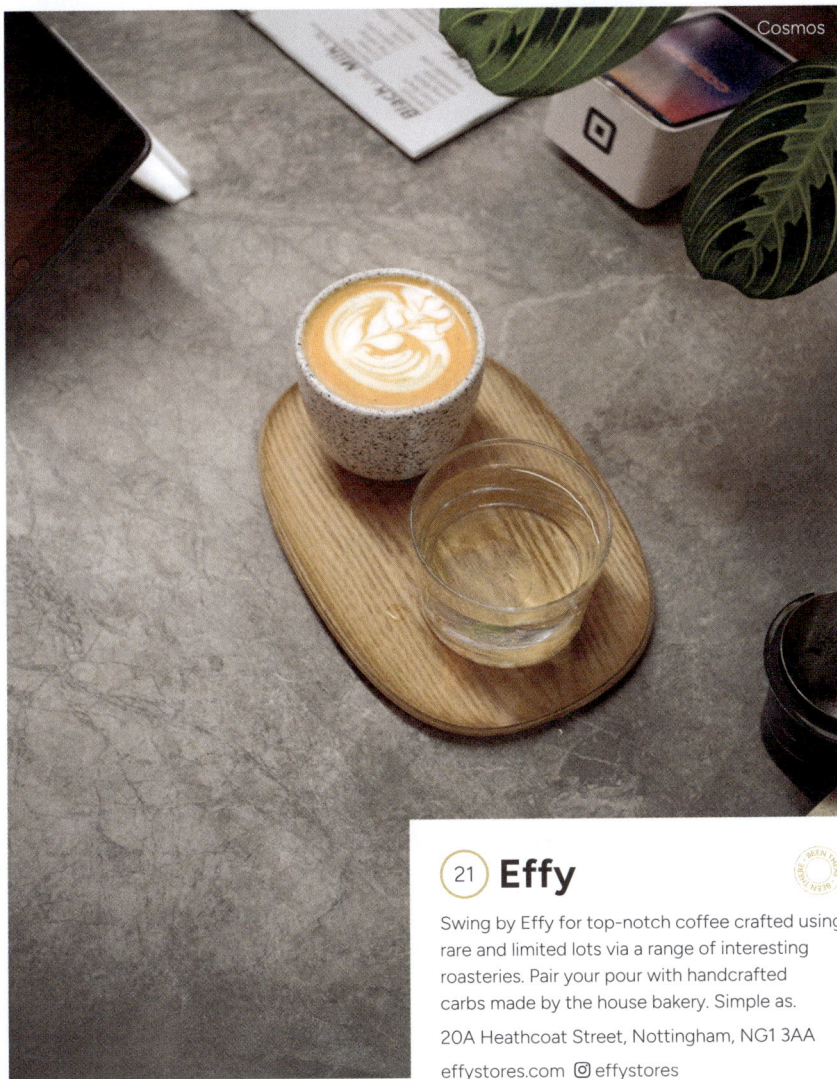
Cosmos

21 Effy

Swing by Effy for top-notch coffee crafted using rare and limited lots via a range of interesting roasteries. Pair your pour with handcrafted carbs made by the house bakery. Simple as.

20A Heathcoat Street, Nottingham, NG1 3AA

effystores.com ⊙ effystores

22 Dispatch

Escape into a Wes Anderson-inspired world at this bubblegum-pink coffee house crafted to represent the director's film of (nearly) the same name. Put more 'French' into *The French Dispatch* experience by pairing your patisserie with a cafetiere of speciality grade coffee.

2 Goosegate, Nottingham, NG1 1FF

dispatchcoffees.co.uk ⊙ dispatchcoffees

23 Cosmos

The Cosmos team are reaching for the stars with an impressive range of coffees available at any one time. The speciality experience may be serious but it isn't po-faced, and includes affogato and cinnamon buns among its attractions.

2 Stoney Street, Nottingham, NG1 1LG

⊙ cosmos_notts

㉔ Lions Cafe

Valley Gate, Sleaford, Lincolnshire, NG34 8YY

lionscafe.co.uk | 01529 417238

Lions Cafe lionscafesleaford

This new addition to Sleaford has kicked off a passion for speciality coffee among previously uninitiated locals, while also scratching the itch for in-the-know residents who now have a place to sink a decent brew with other people who speak their love language (coffee, of course).

The team did their homework by finding the right speciality-grade beans for the job, finally plumping on a seasonal blend that's flame-roasted in small batches especially for them by Lizzie Powell at Coffee Bean Shop. When pulled through the Sanremo Verona and paired with steamed milk – or served black – it's unctuously smooth, balanced in acidity and features a lively aroma while packing notes of chocolate, pecan and jammy sweetness.

Stomach roaring? Add a blueberry or lemon muffin to your breakfast order

Accompanying the java is a comforting breakfast menu of classic cafe fare which honours seasonality and locally sourced produce. Dishes are mixed up to rep the month, but key hero compilations always feature. Get your grill on with the Lion's full English: a trad combo of Lincolnshire sausages, bacon, runny eggs, mushrooms, hash brown, beans and grilled tomato, mopped up by a thick slice of toast. Another fave is the Eggs Hebridean which comprises poached eggs, black pudding and hollandaise sauce on toasted sourdough.

Established
2024

Key roastery
Coffee Bean Shop

Brewing method
Espresso, filter

Machine
Sanremo Verona RS

Grinder
Fiorenzato F64 EVO

Opening hours
Mon-Fri
7am–4pm
Sat
8am–4pm

Norwich Puppet Theatre, St James, Whitefriars, Norwich, Norfolk, NR3 1TN

circushead.co.uk | 07930 164385

 circushead circusheadcic

There's no end to the not-for-profit endeavours of these coffee-loving innovators. The coffee shop, run by volunteer ambulance staff, paramedics and trained baristas, opened in Norwich Puppet Theatre to support the arts as well as ambulance staff's mental health, while serving kick-ass coffee.

The unique setting has undergone a much-needed transformation in recent years and is now the perfect space to bring the local community and NHS ambulance staff together over top-notch brews.

Circus Head uses kindred-spirit roastery Sanctuary – the only UK roastery to share its profits with animal rescues and sanctuaries – as its main bean supplier. A range of other roasteries, such as All Things Bloom, also feature on rotation, appearing mostly – but not exclusively – as V60 and filter.

Circus Head also runs a mobile coffee service, which is available to hire

Proceeds from coffee sales fund important initiatives such as bespoke mental-health projects for struggling or at-risk ambulance staff. There is also the opportunity to buy a paramedic or ambulance staff member a coffee as a show of gratitude and support, via the Bad Day Buttons pay-it-forward scheme. Further projects range from barista training to in-house counselling.

Established
2022

Key roastery
Sanctuary Coffee

Brewing method
Espresso, V60,
Kalita Wave, filter,
batch brew

Machine
Sanremo
Zoe Compact

Grinder
Sanremo X-One

Opening hours
Mon, Fri
10am-2pm
(check socials for opening hours)

26 Fika Norwich

25 Wensum Street, Norwich, Norfolk, NR3 1LA

fikanorwich.co.uk

 fikanorwich fikanorwich

The *'coffee & motivational nonsense'* message on the window of this speciality hangout hints at its relaxed nature, while the sight of owner Mark Lawrence crafting perfect pours using pro coffee kit cements it as a destination for quality brews.

One of the ways Mark has turned Fika Norwich into a community hub is by carefully considering the cafe seating, and stripping out the coffee bar that usually divides customer from barista. It results in conversation – and not always caffeine related – between everyone.

Despite the cafe's elevated coffee offering, there's a pleasing lack of speciality elitism and Mark is always happy to talk through the beans and prep methods available: *'There are no stupid questions about coffee here,'* he says. *'If you don't ask, how will you know?'*. This open attitude also extends to playful coffee creations crafted from sodas – don't knock a Dr Pepper and 'spro shot till you've tried it.

☕ Pair your brew with seasonal bakes like canelés, pistachio cookies and sugar waffles

A close partnership with small-scale Belfast roastery Lucid results in consistently high-quality house beans. The roastery's Colombian Popayan espresso (washed, with notes of mandarin, caramel and vanilla) is a returning favourite and tastes just as delicious black as with milk.

It's also always worth enquiring about the guest roasts: Mark sources rare beans from European roasteries such as Dak, People Possession and Friedhats.

Established
2019

Key roastery
Lucid Coffee Roasters

Brewing method
Espresso,
Kalita Wave,
Moccamaster

Machine
La Marzocco Linea PB

Grinder
Mahlkonig EK43 S,
Anfim SP II+

Opening hours
Mon-Fri
8am-2pm

Norwich

180

27 The Yard Coffee

1a Pivotal House, Orford Yard, Red Lion Street, Norwich, Norfolk, NR1 3TB

theyardcoffee.co.uk | 01603 299034

theyardcoffee the-yard-coffee

Shoppers in Norwich seeking refuge from the hustle and bustle head to the light-filled Pivotal House to satisfy their craving for quality coffee. The Yard is an oasis of calm where both in-house creatives and passersby can take a break and enjoy the kind of chill-time only a well-crafted cup of coffee can provide.

Sit in the airy atrium and savour a toffee-forward flat white made with beans from Suffolk's Crude Coffee Roasters. Or explore the list of rotating guest roasts to sample vibrant fruit and floral flavours – recent favourites have come from Hundred House, Sanctuary, and Rumour Coffee Company. Looking for a quiet escape? Head to The Back Yard to unwind while exploring a drinks menu that includes coffee cocktails, natural wines and craft beers.

☕ The Yard's pistachio iced latte is a Norwich summer staple

Recently upgraded with the addition of a kitchen, the cafe now offers a range of tempting breakfast, brunch and lunch options, providing even more reasons to linger. And if you're not staying for a meal, you should at least sample one of the lush vegan and gluten-free cakes – the seasonal crumble bar is highly recommended.

Established
2021

Key roastery
Crude Coffee
Roasters

Brewing method
Espresso, batch brew,
cold brew

Machine
Conti Monte Carlo

Grinder
Anfim SP II

Opening hours
Mon-Sat
8.30am-5pm
Sun
10am-5pm

Norwich

Pining for that outdoor feeling?

keepcup.com

Certified
(B)
Corporation

1%
FOR THE
PLANET

The Lawn Cafe

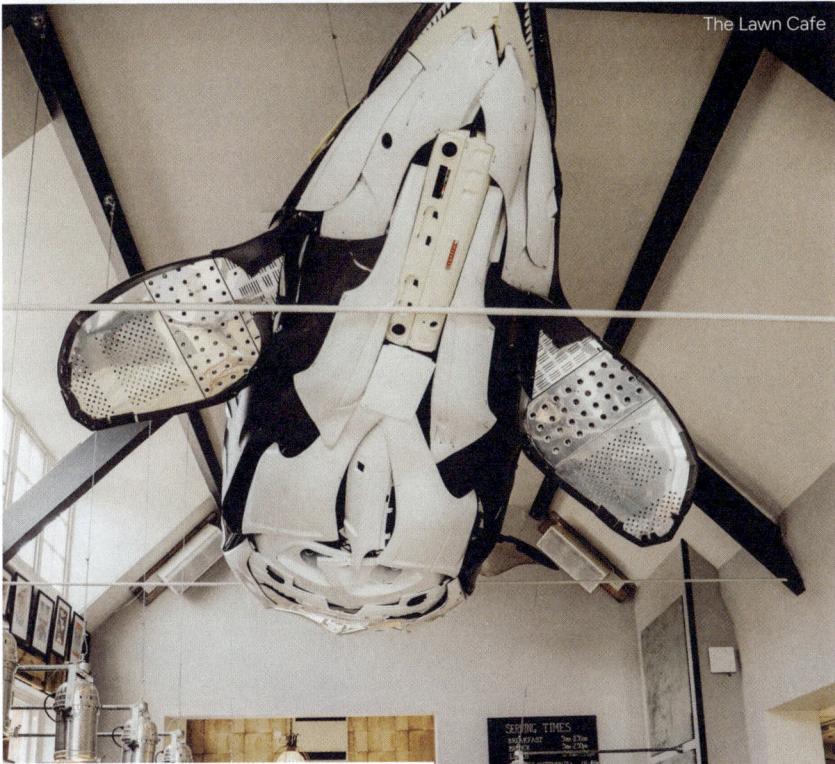

28 The Lawn Cafe

Visit this charming cafe to sip own-roasted coffee care of parent roastery Stokes Tea and Coffee. The cafe, which lies next to Lincoln Castle in the former cookhouse of a Lincoln asylum, is one of a small indie chain and features a flying orca sculpture.

Union Road, Lincoln, LN1 3BU

stokescoffee.com ⊙ stokescoffee ✂

29 Shou Coffee

'Shou' translates as 'observe, guard or serve' in Chinese. Chosen by founding brothers Cal and Ed Cheung it represents the careful craft that goes into their quality coffee offering and Cal's ceramics in which the food and drink are served.

62 High Street, Watton, Norfolk, IP25 6AH

⊙ shou.coffee

30 Flock

This newbie to the Norwich coffee scene has moved into the spot that was previously Littlehaven Coffee Co. and deals in speciality brews, carby treats and feelgood community vibes. Join the locals flocking there for next-gen speciality sips.

45 St Stephens Square, Norwich, NR1 3SS

⊙ flockcoffeehouse

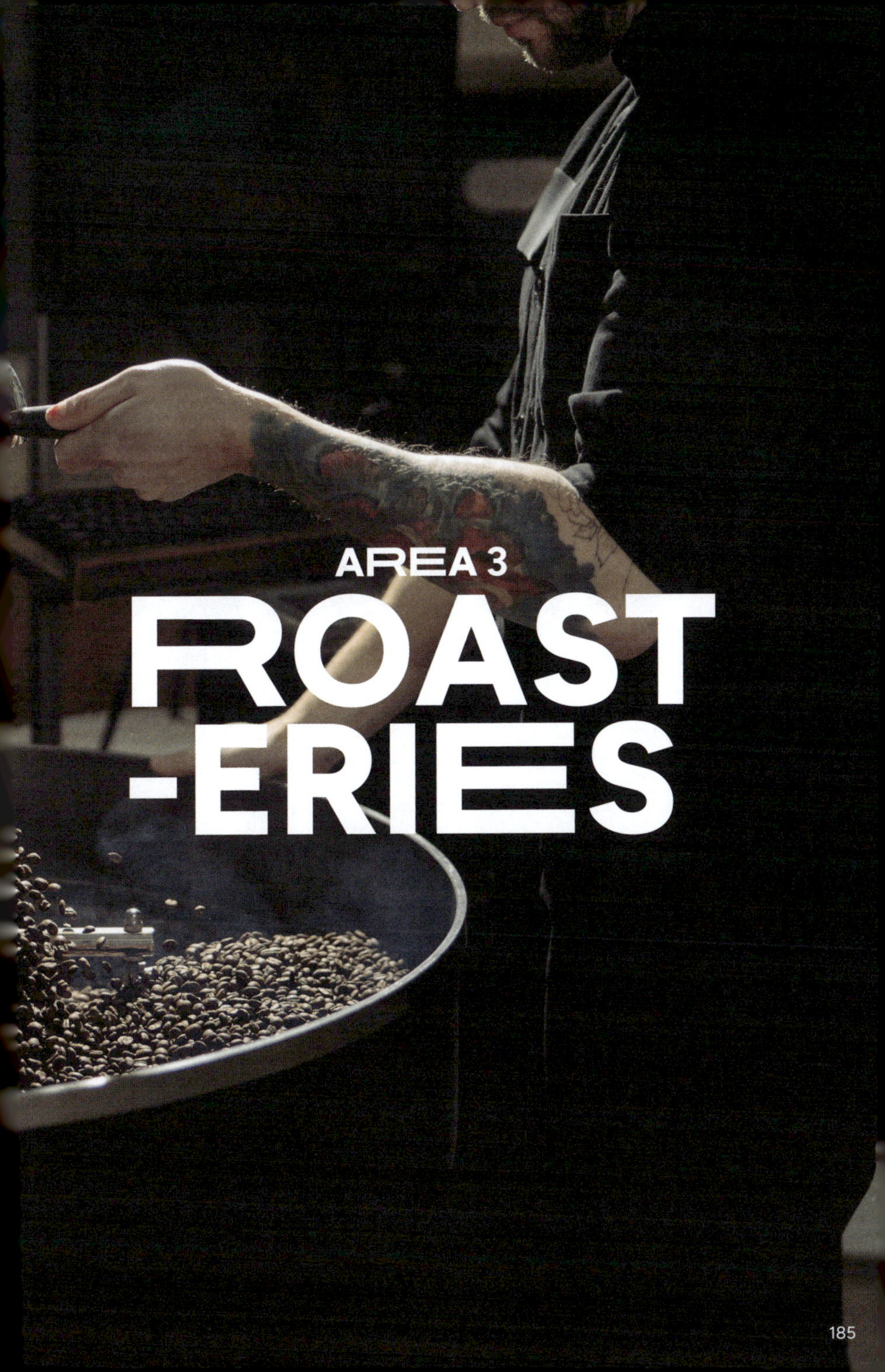

AREA 3
ROAST-ERIES

Hundred House Coffee

SY8 Studios, Gravel Hill, Ludlow, Shropshire, SY8 1QX

hundredhousecoffee.com

f hundredhousecoffee ⦿ hundredhousecoffee

Its track record of producing outstanding coffees and reputation for eye-catching packaging has resulted in Hundred House holding the status of a roasting heavyweight in the Midlands.

Founders Matt Wade and Anabelle De Gersigny have extensive experience in the art world, so supporting creativity was a key consideration when they launched the roastery in 2016. Through their Art + Industry programme they host interactive coffee-event installations, deliver student product-development projects with nearby schools and commission community-led initiatives which celebrate local culture and heritage.

'Coffee-curious connoisseurs will enjoy the Freak & Unique collection of out-of-the-ordinary coffees'

Dive into the Hundred House online shop and you'll find the Great Taste award-winning Bon Bon (a sweet and sticky espresso blend) and Nom Nom (a coffee with 50 per cent less caffeine than the average roast).

Coffee-curious connoisseurs will enjoy the roastery's Freak & Unique collection of out-of-the-ordinary coffees, complete with limited-edition artwork, which can be bought to directly support creative initiatives.

Established
2016

Roaster make & size
Diedrich IR-12 12kg,
Probat P12 12kg

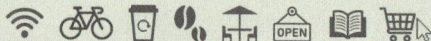

Ludlow

32 Quarter Horse Coffee

10 Kenyon Street, Birmingham, B18 6AR

quarterhorsecoffee.com | 01212 745740

quarterhorsecoffee quarterhorsecoffee

Since 2023, this Birmingham roastery has operated from a large solar-powered premises in the city's buzzing Jewellery Quarter. Inside the high-spec space, the team roast carefully procured beans, utilising a Sovda colour sorter in the production process to screen out defect beans and elevate the overall quality of the coffees.

Coffee lovers can check out the roastery when picking up bags of beans for their home hopper. For further-afield Quarter Horse fans, explore the range via the online shop which stocks a varied stable of coffees, including the bestselling and Great Taste award-winning Dark Horse Espresso and the bright and fruity Roan Espresso house blend.

A popular subscription service offers coffees hailing from a different origin in each monthly drop, all delivered in home-compostable and letterbox-friendly 250g bags. Choose between chocolatey, smooth and sweet notes or the wild, fruity and funky alternative.

'Coffees hailing from a different origin in each monthly drop'

In 2024, the team launched a new training space alongside an expanded barista training programme at their Midlands School of Coffee. Both home brewers and professionals are welcome. Co-founder Nathan Retzer says: *'Our award-winning espresso blends are great for any cafe, restaurant or office and we love working with people who care about coffee as much as we do.'*

Established
2012

Roaster make & size
Giesen W30 30kg,
Stronghold S9X 5kg

Birmingham

187

Courtyard Coffee Roasters

14d High Street, Eccleshall, Staffordshire, ST21 6BZ

courtyardcoffeeroasters.co.uk | 01785 561174

courtyardcoffeeroasters courtyardcoffeeroasters

Courtyard Coffee has been in the roasting game since the early 1980s. While its original roaster has been traded in for a newer model (a cherry-red Diedrich 2.5kg infrared drum machine), the company ethos remains the same: to work exclusively with ethical importers and roast the best beans in small batches.

'Founder David Wiggins allows the beans to fully develop during roasting'

Beans are sourced from Africa, India, Indonesia, and Central and South America for the Courtyard collection of around 20 single-origin arabicas and high-quality blends. Regardless of their country of origin, founder David Wiggins allows the beans to fully develop during roasting to reveal a sweet and toasty medium city-roast.

David is also passionate about crafting a range of decaffeinated beans and there are at least three options available at any time, all of which are water processed.

Beans are available online and on-site, and roastery tours can be booked in advance.

Established
2015

Roaster make & size
Diedrich 2.5kg

34 Stokes Coffee

The Lawn, Union Road, Lincoln, Lincolnshire, LN1 3BU

stokescoffee.com | 01522 523548

stokescoffee stokescoffeeroasters

Robert William Stokes founded this legendary Lincoln coffee company over 120 years ago. Four generations later, his great-grandson Nick Peel continues his legacy by producing high-quality speciality coffees and teas for Stokes' own destination cafes (The Lawn, High Bridge, Welton, Stokes To Go and ultra-modern new spot Newark Café which houses an on-site roaster) and for wholesale customers across the UK.

Stokes' promise of quality beans is backed by a century of roasting experience, and its coffees are the culmination of the passion, pride and dedication of everyone in the supply chain. Stokes' master roasters use their wealth of expertise to bring out the best in every bean using a high-tech Loring Smart Roaster which consumes 80 per cent less natural gas than a typical roaster. One of the newest blends to get a spin in the drum was The Castle Line, crafted especially for Stokes' new cafe in Nottinghamshire.

'Stokes' Zero Waste scheme sees wholesale customers receive orders in reusable buckets'

The team's strong ethical and eco principles have led them to implement initiatives like Zero Waste, where wholesale customers receive orders in reusable buckets. Seven years in, the scheme is still going strong.

Ever evolving, Stokes continues to train the next generation of baristas at its BSA Barista Training Academy. To sample the latest speciality coffees, sign up online for the Roasters Choice and get beans delivered direct to your door.

Established
1902

Roaster make & size
Loring S35
Kestrel 35kg

Lincoln

Butterworth & Son Coffee Roasters

1d Boldero Road, Bury St Edmunds, Suffolk, IP32 7BS

butterworthandson.co.uk | 01284 767969

butterworthandson butterworths

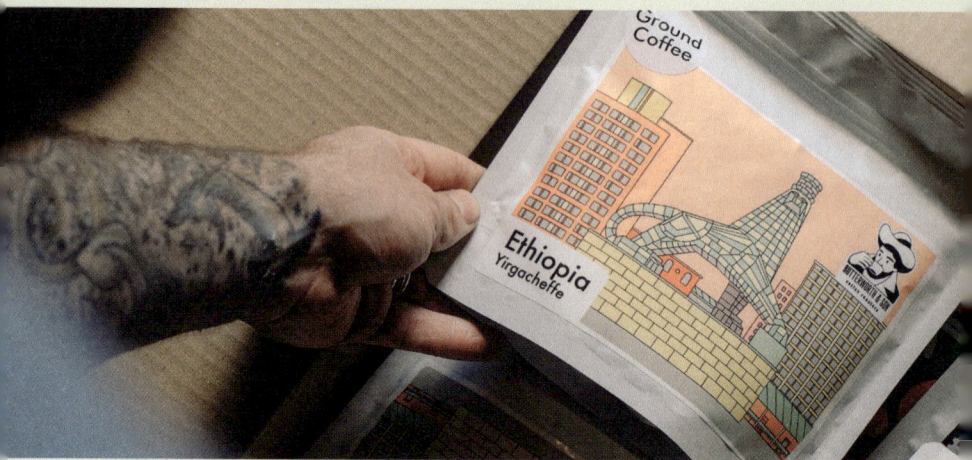

The Butterworth family first made a name for themselves in the 19th century when Harry Butterworth plied his trade as a tea dealer in the Manchester area. Fast forward to 2011 when the family saw the potential for the business to segue into the speciality coffee scene and they jumped into the world of roasting.

Today, the company is one of East Anglia's leading independent coffee roasteries. Butterworth & Son supplies beans to cafes, restaurants and businesses, and offers barista training, equipment servicing, repair, sales and rental. The team also organise annual latte-art throwdowns in Bury St Edmunds and Norwich.

'Regularly travelling across the coffee-growing belt to source top-quality beans'

Rob Butterworth has led the roastery since its inception. His dedication to building strong relationships with smallholders and indigenous communities sees him regularly travelling across the coffee-growing belt to source top-quality beans. As a result, Rob and team offer a wide selection of micro-lot coffees, processed in various ways including washed, honey and natural.

Coffee fans can get a Butterworth & Son fix by buying beans from the website or through various retailers in East Anglia, as well as Selfridges in London. Overwhelmed by the options? A taster pack is the perfect way to sample coffees of various styles and countries of origin.

Established
2011

Roaster make & size
Diedrich IR-23 23kg
Diedrich IR-5 5kg

Bury St Edmunds

Symposium Coffee Roasters

21c Alston Road, Hellesdon Park Industrial Estate, Norwich, NR6 5DS

symposiumcoffee.co.uk

symposium_coffee_roasters

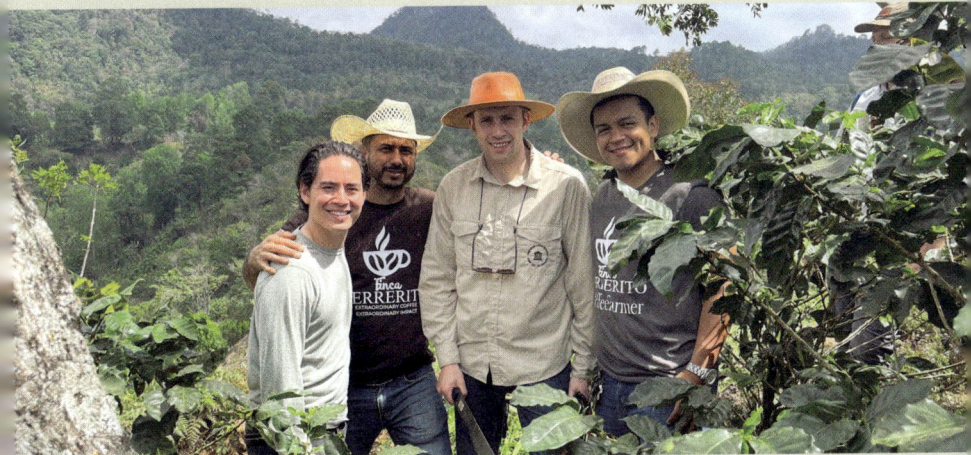

Symposium's commitment to producing high-calibre, environmentally sound coffee that is fully traceable from farm-to-cup has garnered the roastery respect within the speciality coffee scene.

Wife-and-husband team Catriona and Steven Sheard (and their sprocker spaniel Penny) have spent the past half-decade forging lasting relationships with small, family-run coffee farms which put agroforestry and permaculture first.

They share a belief that long-term partnerships, bounded by environmentally friendly practices, lead to better-tasting coffee. That's why Symposium sources greens directly from farmers (many of the coffees come from farms they've visited) before roasting them on a Giesen using clean electric energy.

'This environmental seal of gold-standard approval complements their efforts in sustainable coffee production'

Following a recent trip to see their friends at fifth-generation coffee farm Finca Terrerito in Honduras, Catriona and Steven received news that Symposium is now a Smithsonian Bird Friendly-certified roastery. This environmental seal of gold-standard approval complements their efforts in sustainable coffee production.

While the core range is mostly made up of beans from Central and South America, micro-lots from Africa pop up throughout the year.

Established
2020

Roaster make & size
Giesen W6E 6kg

Norwich

191

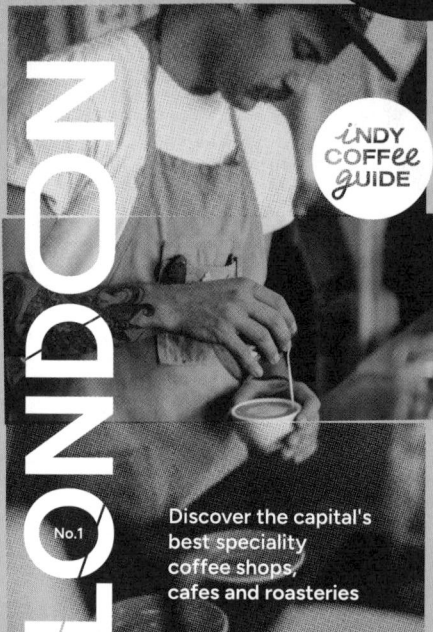

37 Outpost Coffee Roasters

This Nottingham roastery takes a three-pronged approach which focuses on sourcing from standout farmers who are paid a fair price for their beans, roasting to release a kaleidoscope of flavours from those greens, and training baristas to help them coax every delicious note from the beans.

32 Salisbury Square, Nottingham, NG7 2AB

outpost.coffee ◉ outpostcoffeeroasters

38 Norfolk Coffee

This eco-friendly roastery has just moved to a new site where it's cooking up coffee while paying farmers a fair price for fully traceable beans, using compostable coffee bags and carrying out wholesale deliveries in its electric van. Order beans via an online subscription.

White House Farm Barns, Fakenham Road, Pensthorpe, Norfolk, NR21 0LN

norfolk.coffee ◉ norfolkcoffee

39 Strangers Coffee Company

There are lots of ways to make friends with Strangers Coffee in Norwich: watch its beans being roasted through the window of the Dove Street roastery, visit the cafe on Pottergate, hit the wall hatch on All Saints Green or grab a brew from its cart in the menswear department of Jarrolds.

10 Dove Street, Norwich, NR2 1DE

strangerscoffee.com ◉ strangerscoffee

Notes

Somewhere to keep a record of
exceptional beans and brews you've
discovered on your coffee adventures

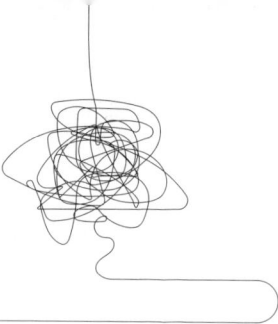

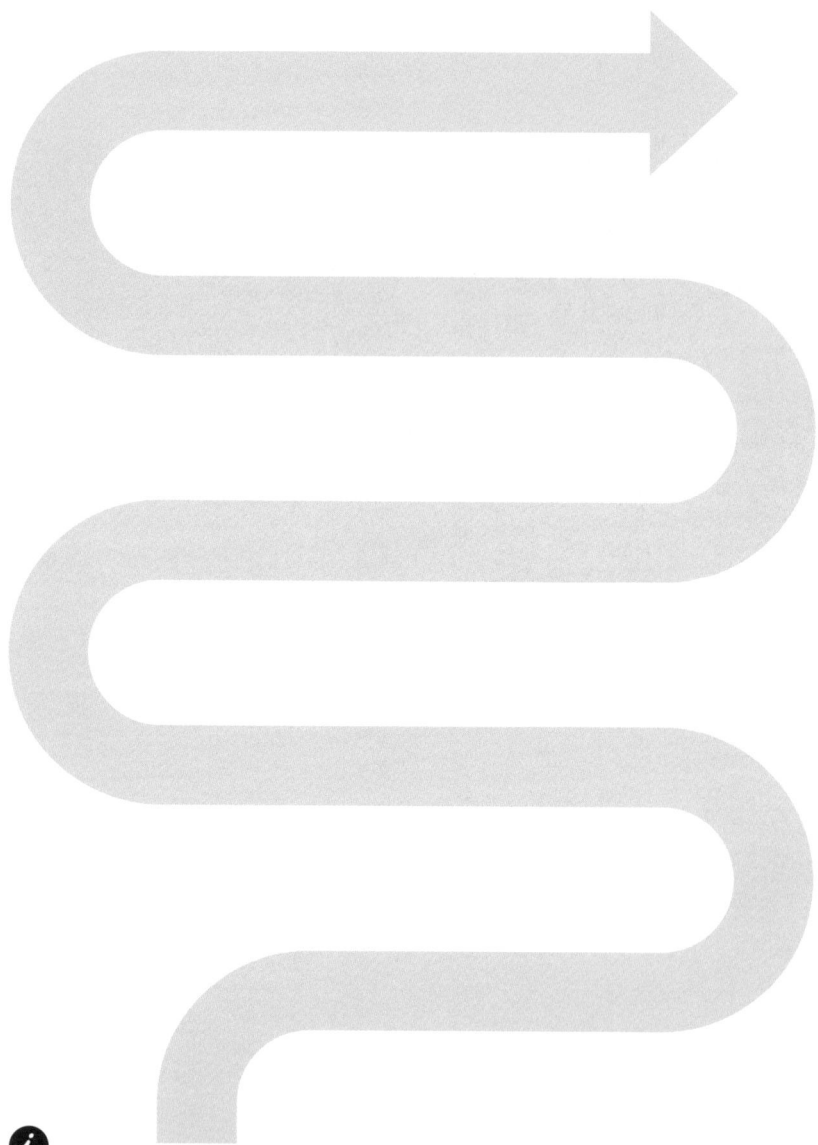

G

H

J

K

L

M

N

O

P

FOR
BREW
FRE
&BEA
GEEK

V
AKS
N
S ...

**iNDY
COFFee
gUIDE**

With the full collection of
Indy Coffee Guides to hand,
you'll always know where
to find the best speciality
coffee in the UK.

Shop the full range, including
guides for London; the South of
England; Wales; and Scotland at

indycoffee.guide